*William Alexander Silverman.*

## William Alexander Silverman

A FIRST-RATE EDITOR and meticulous researcher, William Alexander Silverman began learning the newspaper trade at age sixteen. His first job was with an Altona, Michigan, paper that needed a photographer. Young Silverman bought a camera at a nearby shop and had the clerk show him how to use it. (He was fired after a week.) Later he became a reporter at the *Port Huron Times Herald*. Over the next 15 years Silverman worked at numerous papers, and even started his own paper in Buffalo during the depression.

Silverman rose to chief of the copy desk at the *Detroit Free Press* before he returned to his native Cleveland in 1949 and joined the old *Cleveland News*. When the *News* closed in 1960, Silverman became book editor of the *Detroit News*. Upon his retirement in 1974, he returned to Cleveland and resided there until his death in 1979.

Silverman was a founding member of the Detroit Newspaper Guild, a past president of his American Legion chapter, and a member of Sigma Delta Chi. He also wrote for *True Detective* magazine in his spare time.

Silverman's biggest story in Detroit was a front-page one in August of 1968. In that story, he disputed the origin of a $300,000 picture titled "Young Woman with Violin" because, as both his investigative sense and violin knowledge told him, the bow belonged to a later period of time than the picture claimed.

# The VIOLIN HUNTER

### By
### William Alexander Silverman

### With a foreward by
### Josef Gingold

## PAGANINIANA PUBLICATIONS, INC.
### 211 West Sylvania Avenue,
### Neptune City, N.J. 07753

ISBN 0-87666-577-6

*To*

*my mother, and my wife,*
*the women in my life.*

AN ACKNOWLEDGMENT

I am indebted to many people, attachés of the Italian,
French, and British governments, and especially to
the Fine Arts Division, Cleveland Public Library.

W. A. S.

*Scroll of the ex-Greffuhle violin by Antonio Stradivarius, 1709*

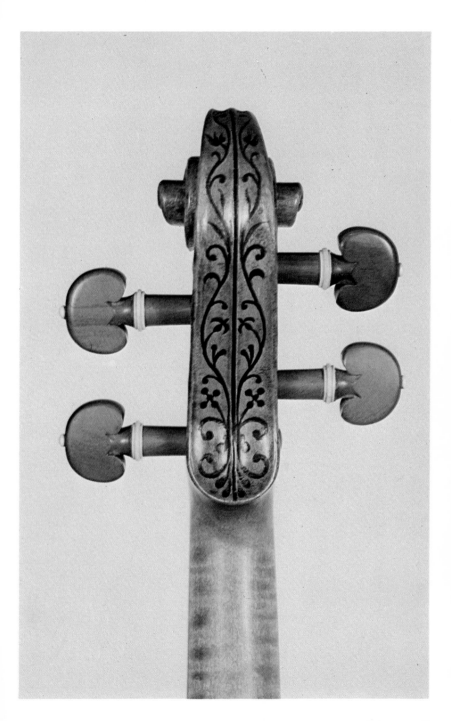

*Another view of the scroll*

# Contents

*The Greffuhle, made for the King of Spain*

*The Greffuhle, probably the first of all decorated instruments*

# FOREWORD

WHEN I FIRST KNEW that the violin would be my life's work, I dreamed of the time when I could own and play upon an instrument from the hands of one of the old Italian masters. As the years went by, and I had the joy of acquiring and playing upon a beautiful Stradivari, a violin made in 1683 and known as the "Martinelli," I realized for the first time the true wonders of the creations fashioned in Cremona: for there is no stringed instrument on earth with a more glorious voice.

Like all musicians, I soon learned that almost inevitably, the man who performs on one of these violins can expect this question: "What is it that makes the violins of old Cremona so wonderful?"

It is an intriguing question, and it has defied all men except possibly one, for more than two hundred years. His name was Luigi Tarisio. Invariably, when the topic comes up, Tarisio's name is mentioned. I soon learned that had it not been for this mysterious man, few if any of us would today have the pleasure of performing upon the instruments created during the golden age of the violin—the days of Stradivari, Amati, Guarneri, and Bergonzi.

I wished to know more of Tarisio, but could find his name in only a few musical dictionaries and books which were largely autobiographies of fiddle dealers. I learned little from these; none of the authors seemed to have known him well, and they were vague in their descriptions of him.

# CHAPTER 1

THE MAN STOOD ALONE on the crest of the hill overlooking Paris. In his tattered clothing he looked like some farmer's scarecrow outlined against the sky. Shapeless clouds drifted by and they were beginning to take on the hues of approaching evening. It had been a warm, bright spring day in 1827.

The scarecrow was thirty-five years old. He stood six feet, but his gaunt figure made him seem even taller. His forehead was the color of copper, and the growth of many weeks bearded his face. He had deep blue eyes—as blue as the sky against which he stood silhouetted. Below him, in the distance, lay the metropolis, stretching as far as he could see.

To this man Paris seemed strange, mysterious, and exotic, its fingers of steel and stone thrust proudly upward; teeming with the movements of thousands upon thousands of people, voicing its life in countless ways. Actually, from his distance, he could hear nothing; but he had thought about Paris for so long, fortifying his imagination with

*Lorenzo Guadagnini, Cremona 1742*

*ex-Arnold Steinhardt, owned by Eli Cantor*

every scrap of information that he could get, that he really
believed he could hear all the noises of the city.

The man sat down, removed two sacks from his back
and gently placed them beside the package he had been
carrying. He pulled off his heavy, ankle-high boots. They
were caked with dust and mud, and he frowned when his
fingers found spots where the soles had worn through.
Luigi Tarisio had arrived at the gates of fame. Somewhere
down in the maze that was Paris lay the Petit Champ and
the citadel he sought, the salon of M. Aldric, famous
throughout Europe as a violinmaker and dealer.

In the sacks he had so carefully put down in the grass
were violin masterpieces from the hands of Antonio Stradivari, Lorenzo Guadagnini, Geofredus Cappa, Joseph Guarneri del Gesu, and Carlo Bergonzi, ten in all; these were
violins that had been "lost" since the middle of the eight-
eenth century and that he himself had discovered.

Even then, in 1827, these violins were worth a small
fortune—especially those by Stradivari, who had made instruments for King James II of England, the Court of
Spain, Pope Benedict XIII, the Duke of Tuscany, the
Grand Duke of Florence, the Czar of Russia, and others of
lesser rank. They had brought large sums of money a hundred years earlier, too, for Stradivari's genius had been
recognized early in his lifetime. But like the physicians of
his time, Stradivari had two fees, a large one for those who
could pay and a small one for his countrymen who loved
the violin but had little money.

Time had not tarnished the fame of Stradivari. On the
contrary, during the ninety years that had intervened between his death in 1737, and this spring day that found
Luigi Tarisio at the edge of Paris, the violins of Cremona,
where Stradivari and his contemporaries had worked,

were coveted more than ever for their clear, strong, melodious voices and superb beauty.

Many other men had made violins, many were still making them, but none even remotely approached the artistry of the violinmakers of Cremona. To say they did would be like comparing a rhinestone to a diamond. What made the Cremona violins of Stradivari's time so great? Was it the wood? The varnish? The skill that went into their creation? No living man knew although many had sought this secret.

Tarisio had left his home in Milan early in February and had walked each step of the way, across the plains of Lombardy, honeycombed with surprising little hills and valleys, dotted with the drab gray of olive orchards. He had strolled through a land of streams, vineyards, waving fields of maize, wood groves and flowers—all in an abundance to dazzle the imagination. He had braved the foothills of the Alps, which had frowned down upon him in all their glacial glory, and even at his distance they had been bleak. The sun had bronzed his face and arms, burning deep lines around his eyes.

He had trudged across the Piedmont, where the cattle seemed thin and rangy, past the scars of war, a ruined house here and there, its roofless walls exposed to the elements. Yesterday, over this same region, had rolled the sound of marching feet, roaring cannon, and the shrieks of the wounded. Now he had seen activity of another kind, the movement of farmers in the field, new growth lifting its head through the sod. He had passed through Varese, and through Arona at the other end of a tranquil little lake, through Lyon and up the plains of middle France. He had slept in barns and sheds, often in the open, and only once in a real bed. That was in Lyon,

*Joseph Guarnerius del Gesu, Cremona 1734*

*ex-Ruggerio Ricci*

where his treasures from Cremona had so captivated Pierre Sylvestre, the French violinmaker, that he had sheltered Tarisio for the night and advised him of the best men to see in Paris. Sylvestre had mentioned M. Aldric, whose clientele was the most exclusive in Europe; J. B. Vuillaume, a man near Tarisio's age but definitely one whose star was rising, and Jacques Pierre Thibout, elder statesman of the Parisian clique which dealt in rare stringed instruments. And now Tarisio had reached the end of the long road. Somehow, on thinking back, it did not seem so far, but his thick beard told him otherwise. He had been clean-shaven the day he left home.

A quarter of a mile away, nestled in a curve in the road, was an inn. Tarisio picked up his treasures, reassured himself by the feel of coin in his pockets, and strode off in quest of a night's rest.

That evening, in the small room he had rented with almost his last coin, and out of habit he had acquired when he was first old enough to begin repeating his mother's nightly prayer, he murmured:

"*Benedic, domine, nos et haec tua dona, quae de tua largitata sumus sumpturi per Christum dominicum nostru.* . . ." "Bless us, oh Lord, and these Thy gifts. . . ."

He crossed himself, and fell asleep.

*Scenes of Paris in early 1800's*

*Antonius Stradivarius, Cremona 1715*

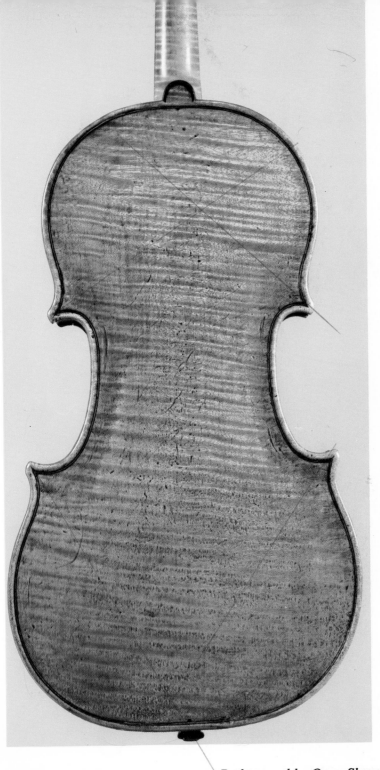

*ex-Rode owned by Oscar Shumsky*

*View of Paris in early 1800's*

# CHAPTER 2

IN THE MORNING, thoroughly rested for the first time in months, Luigi Tarisio looked out upon a sight he never forgot. The city, spread out for miles beneath him, was overwhelming. The months of walking, begging, fiddling for a meal or a chance to lie down in some farmer's barn, had been trying. Yet now he was afraid of Paris—of its vastness and its people. Milan was big, but Paris seemed tremendous. In Italy he was at home and comfortable; he knew his own people and their ways and customs. But in his imagination the French had become strange and mysterious, and there were vague stirrings in his mind that he might be cheated out of his treasures. At that moment, he later confessed to a friend, he thought of turning back and attempting to sell his rare violins to Pierre Sylvestre. Then he realized that he had come so far that it seemed ridiculous to give up now. He squared his shoulders and started down the road, his long legs eating up the distance, the sacks of violins on his back. Doubtless the incongruity of the situation did not occur to him: here were two sacks filled with some of the world's rarest treasures, bobbing like corks on the back of a walking scarecrow.

By noon Tarisio had crossed the Seine over the Pont Neuf. He turned into a little cobblestone street and his eye caught the sign of the Café Momus. A scant hundred yards away stood his destination, the distinguished salon of M. Aldric, to Tarisio the most important person in Europe; for this luthier's clientele was the most exclusive on the continent and his word on violins was law.

For the second time that morning Tarisio felt uncertainty and fear. He hesitated in front of the shop with its gold letters and ornamental grillwork, disturbed by its elegance. He was fully aware of his raggedness. Behind these portals, he knew, was a man whose word would either make him rich, famous, and respected, or send him back to Italy broken and humiliated. Tarisio knew that if Aldric turned him down he would never have the courage to see any of the other dealers in Paris, although on this quest he had staked the efforts of a lifetime.

A passing gendarme gave him a casual glance and grinned, and that was all the reassurance the man from Milan needed. He strode in.

A startled clerk, elegant in long coat and striped trousers, stared incredulously at the apparition that had burst so suddenly into Aldric's cloister-like establishment. His eyes saw only Tarisio's battered boots and tattered clothing—nothing else; not the blazing intensity in the man's face, nor the strong jaw, nor the simple air of dignity. He only saw a bronzed vagabond who literally reeked of the barnyard.

For a moment or two Tarisio merely stood there, not knowing what else to do, giving no explanation of his appearance. He stared at the clerk, fascinated by a perfectly waxed mustache that twitched ludicrously. The clerk stared back into the bluest pair of eyes he had ever seen, and of course there was no way for him to know that this scarecrow was destined to become one of the most fabulous men of his time. The clerk started to call the gendarmes, thought better of it, and stepped hastily into an inner office. Tarisio heard an excited exchange in French, and then Aldric confronted his unheralded visitor.

Tarisio smiled, and a spell seemed to fall upon the place. Then, with the grace of an actor, he opened one of his sacks and took out a Guarneri, holding it aloft by the scroll and bottom in such a way that the light from a window would illuminate it. It was a movement he had rehearsed many times for this precise moment, and he carried it off to perfection. The morning sun, streaming through the windows, splashed over the violin and bathed its brilliant varnish with the fire of diamonds, rubies, and sapphires. Tarisio slowly turned the instrument, letting the sunshine flow across the rich crimson-brown wavy grain in its back, and sparkle mischievously in and around the delicately carved pegs. It caressed the ebony fingerboard with lights and shadows until it looked like a streak of royal velvet.

Aldric stood speechless, and Tarisio, in full command of the situation and with all the skill of a master showman, produced his other treasures—the Stradivaris, the Bergonzi, the Guadagnini and the rest—vanished creations that musicians and patrons of the arts in Europe had hunted for a hundred years; violins the like of which had not been seen in Europe except on rare occasions, and then most often only in the court of a king, a prince, or a cardinal.

There was a question on Aldric's lips, but it was answered before he could utter it.

"I am Luigi Tarisio of Milan," the scarecrow said, "and these instruments are mine."

He laid them on the glass top of a long showcase—on their backs, side by side—and stepped away to watch Aldric gaze upon a sight no other man had yet been privileged to experience; a collection of ten of Cremona's finest masterpieces.

Tarisio himself broke a long silence. "Beautiful, aren't they?"

"Unbelievable," Aldric murmured. "That one on the end, the Stradivari. What is there about that piece of maple and spruce and ebony that says 'the master fashioned me'?"

It was a question Tarisio also had pondered over many times, but had never put into words. But the Frenchman did, and he tried to answer it. The work of Stradivari was like a great statue, he said, which one could contemplate, knowing instinctively by its overpowering beauty that it was the work of the master. The magnificent scroll, its evanescent curves and swells, the beauty and blend of its color—all these things spelled Stradivari, Aldric said. Stradivari was on a level with Titian and Michelangelo in painting and sculpture, with Bach and Beethoven in music, with Balzac and Shakespeare in literature. A connoisseur who looked at a Strad did not have to read the label inside to know, the Frenchman went on, any more than he would have to see a signature on the Madonna del Cardellino to know that Raphael created it.

Then Aldric began to bombard Tarisio with questions. Who was he? Where had he found these extraordinary violins? What did he want for them? The Italian listened patiently, and after Aldric had finished he told his story without embellishment, how he had walked from Milan to Paris, and how he hoped to realize enough from their sale to keep him going.

The two men talked a while longer and finally reached an agreement. Aldric, unable to buy all of the violins himself, proposed to call in some colleagues later in the afternoon. Meanwhile, he would advance Tarisio enough money to buy a new suit and shoes, and to see a barber. Tarisio was agreeable, and soon left with the now impressed clerk as his guide. Strangely enough, he had no hesitation about leaving his treasures behind, for Aldric had won his complete confidence.

That afternoon, bathed and newly clothed, the man from Italy held court in Aldric's salon at an extraordinary meeting of some of Europe's greatest living authorities on violins, summoned hastily to meet Tarisio and bid for his fabulous collection. In addition to Aldric, there were Georges Chanot, Charles François Gand, Jean Baptiste Vuillaume, and several others who for years had sought instruments like these. For hours the men talked excitedly as they examined the Italian's treasures, and at the end of the day, Luigi Tarisio had made his first step toward fame.

Aldric bought six of the violins, Vuillaume two, and Chanot and Gand one each. Aldric bubbled with words. He rubbed his hands gleefully and grabbed Tarisio's coat lapel, talking excitedly of giving him a party at the Frascati Club, a place on the Rue Richelieu where Emerson, the famous English writer, had been just a few days earlier. Vuillaume was amused and Chanot poker-faced. Gand looked at Aldric with amazement as the usually sedate violinmaker and dealer gushed on of women and liveried servants who would tend to Tarisio's every whim. Each of the three was sure that Aldric had failed to discern Tarisio's true character, and they waited for him to commit the final *faux pas*.

"Does Paganini play there?" Tarisio asked soberly.

Aldric laughed. The Frascati Club, he said, was a place like the Palais Royal, or the Cercle des Etrangers, where distinguished people had fun. He was amused at Tarisio's thinking that the maestro performed there. But a moment later Aldric knew that he had made himself ludicrous in the presence of this strange man. He stopped talking and Tarisio, without a word, turned and walked out with Gand, Vuillaume, and Chanot, all carrying the instruments they had bought.

Outside Aldric's salon, Tarisio gazed at the city, seeing it now for the first time. A farmer's donkey-drawn, vegetable-laden cart went by, and an urchin chose that moment to dart across the street, zig-zagging around the donkey, barely missing the prancing feet of a team of horses passing simultaneously in the opposite direction.

Vuillaume, Chanot, and Gand, clutching their precious burdens, stood rooted to the spot in fear because the crash seemed inevitable. But just at the moment it seemed that the child was about to ram head-on into the three Frenchmen, Tarisio's hamlike hand swooped down and plucked the squirming bundle from the street. Frightened, the boy merely stared into Tarisio's face. But the Italian, without a rebuke, thrust a coin into the child's palm and propelled him on his way.

Chanot and Gand excused themselves, and Vuillaume and Tarisio remained to chat. Tarisio explained that he planned to stay in Paris a few days, and when Vuillaume invited him to be his guest, Tarisio accepted at once. This was an unexpected opportunity to broaden his field, for according to Sylvestre, Vuillaume was one of the best-known luthiers in Paris. In fact, Sylvestre's brother Hippolyte had learned violin-making from Vuillaume. And by now, Tarisio had regained his confidence. He no longer suspected all Frenchmen. Arm in arm, the two men strolled down the street toward Vuillaume's home.

Vuillaume lived in semiregal fashion at No. 3 Rue Demours aux Thermes, and although it was some distance away, the afternoon was so lovely that the thought of riding did not occur to either man. On the way Vuillaume told Tarisio about his new salon on the Rue Croix du Petit Champ. At that very moment, he said, it was being prepared for his occupancy. When it was eventually finished, Vuillaume said, it would have tools and equipment for half a dozen apprentices. "My place on the Rue Croix du Petit Champ one day will be the violin capital of Europe," he said confidently. "It will house the rarest Cremonas as well as my own creations."

How true that prediction was, and how vital a role Tarisio himself was to play in it, neither man realized then. Vuillaume had great dreams, and before his career ended he was to become the most prolific violinmaker of all time. More than 3,000 instruments would come from his hands, three times as many as the immortal master of Cremona, Antonio Stradivari, had made.

Two young men—one tall and dark, the other short and blond—strolled on, completely engrossed in their mutual love for stringed musical instruments.

Much later, after dinner and coffee, Vuillaume and Tarisio sat down to talk. Their friendship was beginning.

"Tell me," Vuillaume began, "where and how did you manage to find these violins? What will you do with your money? Are there any more Stradivaris around? And how can I get them?"

Tarisio chuckled. "One question at a time," he replied. "This is a long story." He settled back in his chair, and the first shadows of evening began to stretch over the room. A servant put a log in the fireplace, and as it caught fire, a rash of sparks fell from the grate. It seemed to Vuillaume that a spell had fallen. He waited for Tarisio to speak. This unassuming man, the Frenchman knew, had rediscovered the lost art of the city of Cremona, Italy —the incomparable violins of Stradivari, the Amatis, Bergonzi, and the Guarneris—yet he wore greatness as though it belonged to him. Vuillaume kept his eyes on Tarisio's face, for there was something there that fascinated him.

Tarisio cleared his throat. He felt out of his element, and crossed and uncrossed his legs. He toyed with the knot of a cravat he was unaccustomed to, and stared into the fireplace. "You appreciated the violins I have brought to Paris, M. Vuillaume?" he blurted suddenly.

The question took Vuillaume so by surprise that all he could do was smile. Then, sensing his guest's nervousness, he walked over to Tarisio, patted him on the shoulder, and said: "Today you have made history. Tell me about yourself—how you found these violins and how you began this enchanting quest."

The clock on Vuillaume's mantel ticked noisily, and Tarisio, his voice low, began his story. He spoke haltingly at first, and then, his confidence growing, let it pour out.

Vuillaume sat there, fascinated into silence, feeling the full drama as Tarisio lifted the curtain behind which the art and history of Cremona had been hidden for a century.

*Paris street, about 1830*

*View of Cremona*

# CHAPTER 3

L UIGI TARISIO ALWAYS BELIEVED that God had guided his feet to the churches and farmhouses in Italy where he found his Cremona violins, and that God had given him the gift of recognizing the works of Antonio Stradivari and his great contemporaries. In fact, he had no other explanation for his strange career. He believed, too, that the Lord had endowed him with the gentleness and persistence so necessary to his quest. He believed these things even as he believed that he had been born with a great love for stringed instruments. And the pattern of his life was laid out for him sixteen years before he was born in Milan in 1792.

The year 1776 was a time of unrest and fear. Cremona was preoccupied with many things, and was experiencing fears and uncertainty similar to those of far-off America. Though the Cremonese had long since paid off the enormous Austrian tax of eleven million francs levied to fortify the castle of Santa Croce on the outskirts of their city, the hundred heavy guns still kept an intimidating vigil there. The unpopular Austrian Emperor, Joseph II, faced war with Prussia over the issue of Bavaria. There were rumors of impending trouble with the Turks. All these problems cast their shadows upon Cremona. And times were not good, despite some prosperity, for Cremona now had a mayor and a council; these were men inexperienced in politics and unaccustomed to their power, and they managed affairs poorly.

Antonio Stradivari had been dead for thirty-nine years, and was all but forgotten. Nearly every other day, it seemed, Paolo Stradivari, fanatically devoted to his father's memory, buttonholed a councilman. The City of Cremona, Paolo insisted, could easily afford to buy the home of Antonio Stradivari for a museum. Paolo Stradivari had sound arguments to advance. First of all, the Stradivari family still owned the imposing three-story building in the Piazza San Domenico where Stradivari had created his violins. Second, some of the family were interred in the Chapel of the Rosary directly across the street. San Domenico Church, of which the chapel was but a small part, had long been one of Italy's most imposing church buildings. What more perfect setting for such a museum could there be?

Paolo had pointed out to the councilmen that his father bore one of the most noted names in Cremona's history. He was sure that some day Cremona, because of his work, would become a world center of art. He offered to endow the museum with almost eighty of his father's instruments, as well as with other historic relics: an old family Bible reputed to contain, on the flyleaf, the exact formula of Stradivari's varnish; tools, patterns, and documents, many of which bore the names of kings, emperors, dukes, and princes, and even of a pope.

Paolo Stradivari had not been alone in these arguments.

His brother Giuseppe, a priest and four years his senior, likewise had pleaded with the mayor and councilmen to act, and so had Paolo's children, Antonio 2nd, newly married at thirty-six; Paolo 2nd, thirty years old and his father's assistant in the cloth-exporting business; and his thirty-five-year-old daughter Francesca, a spinster about to enter her novitiate. A few of the councilmen had been vehement in their refusal. Some had doubted the sincerity of the Stradivari family, pointing out that Paolo had thought so little of his father's home as to rent it to the Bergonzis, rival violinmakers, for more than a decade.

In 1776 the affairs of the Stradivari family seemed headed for a crisis. Paolo had sold ten of his father's finest works to a Florentine nobleman, Count Cozio di Salabue. There had been a curious aspect to that transaction because the Count, for some reason desiring anonymity, had made the purchase through the firm of Anselmo di Briati, of Cassle, a small city on the River Po. The Cassle firm, in turn, had acted for a firm in Florence, the Count's true agents.

Some months later, the Count's agents had written to Paolo Stradivari inquiring if he would part with his father's patterns, moulds, and tools. The letter lay unanswered.

Then one afternoon Paolo Stradivari came home from another aggravatingly futile talk with the authorities. This time his despair was great, and his defeat final. A councilman had told him that not only would Cremona refuse to entertain the thought of a Stradivari memorial, but that he himself would use his influence to see that the magnificent San Domenico Church was razed to the ground. The site, he thought, could better serve the citizens of Cremona as a playground or park than as a church now

scarcely used and rapidly falling into decay. This was
Paolo's final blow.

On May 4, 1776, the little cloth merchant, now sixty-
eight years old, sat down and composed the following
letter to the firm of Anselmo di Briati:

> I have already told you that I have no objection to sell
> all those patterns, measures, and tools which I happen to
> have in my possession, provided that they do not remain in
> Cremona, and you will recollect that I have shown you all
> the tools I have, and also the box containing the patterns.
> I place all at your disposal, and as it is simply a friendly
> matter, I will give you everything for twenty-eight giliatis.

The giliati, at that time, was a Tuscan gold coin bearing the coat of arms of Florence, the equivalent then of
9s., 6½d., British.

Paolo's offer to sell for twenty-eight giliatis was turned
down and the Count's agents made a counteroffer of only
five giliatis.

On June 4, 1776, Paolo wrote again to the Cassle company:

> Putting ceremony aside, I write in a mercantile style. I
> see from your favour of the 13th ultimo, which I only re-
> ceived by the last courier, that you offer me five giliatis for
> all the patterns and moulds which I happen to possess, as
> well as those lent to Bergonzi, and also for the tools of the
> trade of my late father; but this is too little; however, to
> show you the desire I have to please you, and in order that
> not a single thing belonging to my father remain in Cre-
> mona, I will part with them for six giliatis, providing that
> you pay them at once into the hands of Domenico Dupuy
> & Sons, silk stocking manufacturers. I will send you all the
> things above mentioned, conditionally that I keep the five
> giliatis and use the other one to defray expenses for the case,
> the packing, and the custom house duty, which will be nec-

essary to send them, and I shall let you have back through Messrs. Dupuy, residing under the market Arcades in Turin, any balance that should remain or (if you like) you may pay the said Messrs. Dupuy seven giliatis, and I shall then defray all the expenses, and send also the two snake-wood bows which I possess.

In Cremona, there was more talk of tearing down the church of San Domenico, and life in Paolo Stradivari's home grew increasingly depressing. He hastened in his efforts to move his father's treasures somewhere away from a city he felt unworthy of them.

Negotiations with Count Cozio's agents speeded up. On July 10th Paolo wrote again.

We learn from Messrs. Dupuy of the receipt of seven giliatis, which you have paid on our account. I have, however, to mention that I did not think I possessed so many things as I have found. It being according to what has been promised, it cannot be discussed over again. It will be a very heavy case, on account of the quantity of patterns and tools, and consequently it will be dangerous to put the violins in the same package.

The violins referred to were several the firm had bought in Cremona from someone else, but which they wished shipped along with Stradivari's things. The letter continued:

I fear without care they will let it fall in unloading it, and the violins will be damaged; I inform you therefore of the fact. You must let me know how I have to send the case. If by land, through the firm of Taborini, of Piacenza, or to take the opportunity of sending it by the Po.

The deal was completed and Antonio Stradivari's tools were consigned to the care of a bargemaster on the River Po named Gobbi.

Cremona had lost some of its finest treasures. Only a few of the master's violins remained in the city. One of these was Stradivari's masterpiece, a violin so perfect that in the future men would refer to it as Le Messie. It hung on the wall in Paolo Stradivari's home in all its varnished glory, a work of matchless beauty.

Paolo Stradivari became ill, and then his wife was stricken. She died in September, 1776, but Paolo lingered.

More letters came from Count Cozio, who wanted the rest of Stradivari's violins, but Paolo, too ill to reply, ignored them. Finally, early in October, Paolo's two sons and his daughter were summoned to his bedside. He told his son Paolo 2nd to carry on his cloth business. He asked Antonio 2nd to complete the sale of the violins to Count Cozio and see that the last of the treasures were taken out of Cremona. To his daughter Francesca he wished success in her career in the church, and in return Francesca promised to pray that some day the world might recognize her grandfather's great art.

This was the last time the family was together. On October ninth, 1776, bitter and disillusioned, Paolo Stradivari died. Francesca became a nun in the church of Saint Sigismondo just outside of Cremona. Antonio 2nd carried out his father's final wishes. In 1777 he sold his grandfather's house to Signor Giovanni Ancina, also sold every violin, except one which Francesca took with her. He even sold Le Messie. Thus was the pattern laid for the career of a man not yet born. Some years later, that man, still very young, eager-faced and full of questions, came to Cremona to find the home of a genius. He inquired in the city and someone sent him to see the Bergonzis, Benedetto and Carlo 2nd, grandsons of Carlo Bergonzi, Stradivari's noted contemporary. They had spent their childhood in the home once occupied by Antonio Stradivari. They took the young visitor through the building and showed him where Cremona's great artist had worked. They told him about Paolo Stradivari and his futile campaign. They told him about Le Messie, because they had seen it often, hanging on the wall of Paolo's home. They told him about Sister Francesca, and the promise she had made to her father, and in the eyes of young Luigi Tarisio they could read a purpose.

*House and workshop of Stradivari*

*More modern view of Stradivari's house*

# CHAPTER 4

THE YEAR WAS 1809, and it was early fall. In the parish of Saint Sigismondo, a few miles from Cremona, nearly everyone was observing Holy Saturday, a day to give thanks to the bounty of the Lord and to celebrate the success of the year's crops. The children of Lombardy were no different from those of other provinces; having paid their respects to their Creator, they felt free to demonstrate their pleasure at their own accomplishments. The grape crops that year had been spectacular.

Ever since nine o'clock in the morning the tiny square in front of Saint Sigismondo had been black with people. The sun shone with brilliance, permeating every fibre of one's body. Though it was still mid-morning, the cobblestones seemed to direct the sun's rays back to one's feet and legs.

A tall, rugged-looking, but not handsome youth of seventeen, carrying a violin and bow wrapped in velvet, walked nimbly through the crowd, sidestepping the jostling elbows.

Tonight he intended to fiddle, sing, and dance, but at

the moment his eyes were fixed on the church; for such a festival was new to Luigi Tarisio.

For two days he had been hiking from Milan, and now, excited by the occasion, he could look only at the church, which was the center of all activity. Before its front doors the crowd seemed to respect a large space; no one ventured beyond an imaginary barrier. Tarisio wriggled through the crowd to this invisible stopping point and waited.

A strange mass stood in the middle of this space, an enormous, octagon-shaped chariot painted deep brown, and hung with volutes of many colors. A wire stretched from its top to the doorway of the church and then vanished inside.

Tarisio followed the wire into the church, where, beneath the high, vaulted roof he saw people walking about as if they were in the street. They talked and laughed. This seemed very strange to the young man, for to him church had always meant hushed restraint. The nave had become an amusement hall, the cloistered foyer with its receptacles of holy water a gathering place for lovers. In a little while the Colombina, an artificial bird made of grain and fireworks, would be set afire, and it was considered a stroke of luck if one could touch its flame.

Though puzzled by the turmoil in these sacred confines, Tarisio was not troubled; he knew his own people, and he knew that these Italians, their prayers finished, were no longer aware of the sacred enclosures, and that in their hearts was no disrespect.

A small boy came in rolling a hoop. Behind him there was a sudden stir, and Tarisio turned in time to see a horse standing contentedly in the shade inside the church entrance. Now the crowd moved in closer to see the Co-

lombina set afire, and Saint Sigismondo no longer was the
church in which one had come to God; it was only the
place that sheltered the bird with the fire. It was cold,
and some in the crowd even wore their hats. The nave
was jammed. Tarisio's eyes followed the iron wire, which
ended on a wooden post at the foot of the altar.

The crowd kept pouring in, climbing upon chairs and
benches, and in the midst of this turmoil, the divine offices
of Christ went on with the Latin cadences of the priests
and the thin voices of the choir boys hopelessly overwhelmed. The people neither saw nor seemed to understand their ancient beliefs. They knew but one thing—this
was the day when the Lord, to make Himself manifest to
others besides the robed monks, took the form of the flaming Colombina. And this the peasants wanted to see. As
the hour approached, all eyes turned to the altar and to
the dove.

The bells struck noon. The celebrant at the altar, in a
piercing voice, cried: "Gloria!" Then he touched a burning torch to the object on the wire. The dove quickened,
its fire crackling, its wings open, and zoomed along the
wire, the golden bundle of grain which formed the tail
sputtering like fireworks.

Between the two rows of humanity it sped toward the
door. Many arms reached up, among them Tarisio's. His
hands passed completely through the flame, and he was
happy. For this, everyone had said, was the pinnacle of
good fortune. Outdoors, as the magic bird approached
the end of its trail, there was a rising wave of sound, a
frantic greeting from the throng. The bird reached the end
of the wire and exploded into nothing. Inside the church,
joy reigned unbounded. The Lord had made Himself
known.

In the midst of the confusion Tarisio had the strange feeling that a pair of eyes were boring through him. Almost fearfully, he looked around, but no one seemed to be paying him the least bit of attention; and then, as though drawn by a magnet, he raised his view to the balcony above the nave. Erect at the rail stood a nun, and Tarisio was aware then that she had been watching him ever since his hands had passed through the flame of the Colombina.

He felt quite calm and comfortable. The ache in his legs, caused by many miles of walking, had vanished. His thoughts became clear. As far as he was concerned, the babel and confusion had ceased to exist, and he stood alone in the center of the nave.

Gradually his eyes became adjusted to the distance and the figure standing on the balcony came into sharper focus: he saw that the nun was smiling. Her features were regular and she had beautiful eyes. Her nose was long and straight, and in her chin and jaw were strength. Then sadness came over Tarisio, for he saw that this woman was old—very old, in his eyes—perhaps in her late sixties or early seventies, but more than that, old far beyond her years. After a moment a monk joined her at the rail, and both stared down at Tarisio. The nun was talking, the monk nodding in agreement.

Someone slapped Tarisio on the back, reminding him that it was time to go outside and fiddle for the dance. He took in the figure of a grinning peasant, and the nun's spell was broken. He glanced back at the balcony. The nun nodded, smiling.

Alternately laughing and singing, Tarisio ran from the church to join the happy throngs outside. Someone led four white oxen to the chariot in the square, hitched them up, and the strange cargo lumbered off to a safe distance from the church. The fireworks were lighted and the booming, crackling roar of gunpowder saluted the square. Someone had a concertina, another a flute. Tarisio tucked his violin under his chin and played like one possessed.

*Cremona as seen from outside the city*

*Portrait thought to be of Stradivari*

# CHAPTER 5

AFTER A WHILE a peasant came to Tarisio and admonished him to play well, because illustrious ears would be listening. The most important nun in the parish, Tarisio was told, was Sister Francesca, granddaughter of the famous violinmaker of Cremona, Antonio Stradivari.

Tarisio guessed then the identity of the nun who had been watching him. He wondered for a moment why Sister Francesca should have been staring at him, and he would have pursued the point, but the peasant stepped away and was quickly lost in the crowd.

In the corner of the square two large barrels of wine—red wine made in Lombardy—became the center of attraction. Someone lifted a leather flacon of white Chianti and a roar of derision went up from the men nearby. "Tuscany wine, throw him out!" The man, laughing gleefully at his joke, spilled the Chianti on the cobblestones, and the dry earth between the stones soaked it up.

"Inferno, Grumello," the men shouted, and Lombardy's wine, rich, red, dry, and heady, flowed like water.

Tarisio played on. A man added the voice of a guitar

to the music. Pretty little girls in bright-yellow blouses and short, flaming-red skirts, pirouetted around the musicians. The afternoon sped by, and one by one the little paper lanterns strung across the square were lighted.

A monk touched Tarisio's arm, and said that Sister Francesca had sent him to fetch the young man. There was a question in Tarisio's face, and the monk hastened to explain. First, Tarisio's hands had passed through the flame of the Colombina. That was a good sign. Second, she had heard of his passion for violins.

"I was in Cremona, just yesterday," Tarisio cried. "I even saw her grandfather's home!"

"I know," the monk replied. "We heard."

He took Tarisio by the arm and guided him through the crowd. Dusk was falling on the cobblestone square. The sky darkened, and the copper beauty of the church spire, which only a short time ago had glistened against a field of azure blue, began to blend into the background.

Everywhere the flame was put to dozens of tightly wound grain torches, adding their brilliance to the strings of glowing paper lanterns. Their flickering light threw distorted shadows against the church. The two men walked along the side of the church till they came to a large oak door, edged with wide bands of hammered bronze. Tarisio's companion lifted the brass latch and the door opened noiselessly. Bright light flowed out into the darkness. Tarisio blinked and, prompted by the pressure on his arm, stepped into a long corridor.

There was a mustiness which told him that this section of the church was seldom used. At the end of the hall another ponderous oak door opened off the left wall. The monk rapped smartly and it swung open, admitting them into an office-like room adorned liberally with the symbols of religion.

Sister Francesca, the picture of serenity, sat behind a flat walnut desk, smiling at the two men. "Thank you, Brother Cosimo," she said to the monk, and then turned to Tarisio: "Sit down, please, in front of me."

As the monk withdrew discreetly to another part of the room, Tarisio noticed a frieze on the wall behind Sister Francesca. Done in rich, warm colors, it depicted a thin, ascetic-looking man with coal-black eyes and snow-white hair, obviously tall, although seated at a bench. He was carving a rectangular block of wood into the scroll of a violin. His fingers were long and slender, like an artist's. Tarisio's eyes strayed to the nun's hands entwined in the rosary on her desk, and he saw a resemblance. The rest of the frieze was a familiar street scene—people and traffic—dominated by a stately three-story frame building. This was the home of Stradivari, the building he had been through only yesterday.

"Do you like it?" the nun asked.

"Oh, yes," Tarisio answered, disconcerted by the nun's direct gaze. He was ill at ease, not accustomed to such penetrating inspection. He felt like what he was, a simple peasant with a love of music, and such close contact with one of the cloth was something he had never hoped for. The presence of this holy woman awed him, and he fidgeted in his chair, twisting and untwisting his hands.

"Brother Cosimo has told you why I wanted to meet you," the nun said. "It seems to me that you are a young man of fortitude. Tell me, will you become a violinist?"

The question startled Tarisio. "Me—a violinist?" The idea had never occurred to him. He shook his head from side to side and spread his hands on the desk, palms down.

The nun saw what he meant. These fingers, crippled and disfigured, would never master any musical instrument. They might be adequate for simple tunes on the violin, but for nothing else. "But I can fiddle a little bit," Tarisio explained. "And I do have a purpose in life—a great purpose."

"Surely it must be a great purpose, and it is one in which you shall succeed, God willing."

The tranquillity in Sister Francesca's voice put Tarisio at ease. He spoke of his hopes and dreams. He held up his left hand to show the nun that his little finger was so stiff —a stiffness he had known since infancy—that he could scarcely bend it. There could be no harmonics in his playing; no trills in thirds, nor sixths, nor octaves, the very core of artistic technique.

When he was seven or eight his mother had wanted him to become another Tartini, a Corelli, or a Pugnani. She often had spoken of Viotti, the son of a blacksmith, who, though still very young, already was a famous violinist. Tarisio had taken lessons on the violin in Milan but after a few months, when the full handicap of his crippled little finger became apparent, his professor sat him in a chair one day and patiently explained why Tarisio could never become an artist.

The professor owned a fine Stradivari, and as Tarisio sat there crest-fallen, the old man gently began to speak of Stradivari. Someday, the professor said, Tarisio might go to Cremona and visit the cradle of the art of violin-making.

"There are too few of these beautiful violins left," the old man had said. "Perhaps there lies your destiny—in finding them."

The seed had been planted, and it grew little by little

until by the time the boy reached his teens, it had become the ambition of his life.

The fabric of man's life is a cloth of countless threads; and for Tarisio it became a garment of many hues. As a very small boy his father had taught him the trade of carpentry and his mother had given him violin lessons. By the time he was twelve or thirteen he was building picnic tables and outdoor benches, much in use in rural Italy at that time, and he also was playing the violin at village festivities.

The things a young boy hears make lasting impressions upon his mind, and Tarisio was a good listener. He often heard the villagers talk about how Napoleon, not too long before, had ransacked Italy for her art treasures. He heard the villagers mutter indignantly how Napoleon had even put on a high art exhibition in France with their treasures, how he had taken the famous bronze-gilt horses from Saint Marco in Venice; how he had stolen the Apollo Belvedere, the Cupid and Psyche from Rome, and the beloved Raphael's Transfiguration. The fact that Italian art had become the rage in Paris was no consolation to these people.

Italians loved music, and the violin was popular and cheap. In Germany whole villages were engaged in turning out violins on a mass-production basis, instruments one could buy for a few copper coins. Occasionally someone would talk of Italy's contribution to the art of violinmaking, but always it was about the long-gone makers of Milan—Paolo Grancino, Giovanni Baptiste Grancino and other members of the Grancino family; Montagazza, Carlo Landolfi, and Testator II Vecchio, one of the earliest violinmakers in history who worked around the year 1510 A.D.

As he grew older Tarisio learned about Cremona and her illustrious makers and it seemed strange to him that hardly anyone ever spoke of them. But in his cunning mind an idea had begun to take shape: If Italian art could become the rage in Europe, why not old Italian violins? Someday, he now told Sister Francesca, he hoped to find all of the wonderful instruments made in Cremona so long ago, and see that they reached the hands of Europe's artists.

A look now passed between the nun and Brother Cosimo, who had stepped back to the desk. It was a look that seemed to electrify the atmosphere of the dignified office.

"Have I said something wrong?" Tarisio asked.

Sister Francesca shook her head, and the sadness in her face deepened. She seemed so old—far older than when Tarisio had first sat down.

She crossed herself, and murmured: *"Vivit post funera virtus*—virtue survives the grave." And she told Tarisio a story he never forgot. Many years ago her illustrious grandfather had a friend in Cremona—the monk Don Desidero Arisi. She had never known her grandfather because he had died three years before she was born. But when she was young, Arisi, and her uncle Giuseppe, also a cleric, had told her many stories about her grandfather and his mastery of the art of violin-making.

As time went on, the fine violins made by Stradivari and other great men in Cremona began to disappear. The two priests often voiced the fear that this art might soon die. The priests, her father, and others in her family had, in later years, tried to interest the city in perpetuating the art, but their efforts had been in vain.

The monk Arisi, Sister Francesca went on, had told her that someday these wondrous instruments would reappear, that perhaps some person would come along and lead a renaissance of the violin. Sister Francesca believed this, and said so, and left no doubt that she thought Tarisio was that person.

"But I am apprenticed to a carpenter in Milan until I reach twenty-five," Tarisio protested. He made it plain how burdensome apprenticeship could be. Even now he was away without consent, and he shuddered to think of his punishment when he returned.

"You need not worry about the apprenticeship," Sister Francesca replied. "Here in the church there are ways of settling such affairs."

She urged him to concentrate upon what she had to tell him. If he were diligent he would find abandoned Stradivari violins in nearly every monastery and church in Italy, in farmhouses, and elsewhere. She had heard of six in the Castle Corte Reale in Mantua, the ancestral home of the Gonzagas, who once maintained their own private orchestra. She urged him to look in the pawnshops, and among the effects of musicians long dead.

There was one violin in particular that he must get, Sister Francesca continued: her grandfather's most perfect piece of workmanship, a violin called Le Messie—the Messiah—because of its perfection. It was a violin she had often seen in her father's home. The varnish was so beautiful that it resembled a painting, a glittering combination of blood-reds, browns, and yellows, all mixed in a manner to defy description. And though it was now more than a hundred years old, it would appear as if varnished just the day before. This violin undoubtedly was in the hands of a nobleman in Florence, she said, Count Cozio di Salabue, who operated a business firm clandestinely.

Tarisio seemed shocked. The idea of a nobleman in

commerce was something he had never heard of before. Sister Francesca correctly interpreted the astonishment on his face and explained that in these days it was not unusual. Many of Italy's noble families were in difficult circumstances and some had turned their hands to business.

From somewhere in the church came the muffled chimes of nine o'clock. Sister Francesca arose, bade her guest good night, and walked sedately out of the room.

Outdoors, the dancing and singing continued, and one by one the torches began to flicker out. Darkness covered most of the church grounds, but in the courtyard a large group still continued its fun. Father Cosimo and Tarisio passed the celebrants on the way to the monk's dormitory. They reached it and walked into a room with a score of small bunks. Tarisio dropped off to deep sleep almost instantly and dreamed that he was a knight in armor riding a huge white horse, and that his duty was to gallop constantly over every hill and dale in Italy. It seemed as though he had just fallen asleep when he was awakened by a gentle hand on his shoulder. Sunshine was streaming through the windows. Tarisio looked up into the face of the monk and sensed that something was wrong.

Sister Francesca had passed away during the night, the monk told him, but after she had left Tarisio she had written to the Bishop of Milan urging him to terminate Tarisio's apprenticeship. That the Bishop would honor this request was practically certain, the monk said. He reached into his tunic and brought out a folded square of parchment, which he opened to its full proportions. It was Sister Francesca's letter. The monk began to read:

To His Holiness, Bishop of Milan, Italy, Anno Christi, 1809
Most Reverend Father:
  The bearer is Luigi Tarisio, of Milan, who is apprenticed

to a carpenter in your diocese. A noble burden has been thrust upon this youth's shoulders; his heart and mind are dedicated to the task of restoring to mankind the treasured creations of my illustrious grandfather, Antonio Stradivari. In our land, torn and bleeding from the wounds of internecine war, sadness and despair have become an intaglio symbolical of all that is evil and bad. The songs and music have vanished from the hearts of our beloved children. The glorious violins and cellos of my grandfather, endowed with an almost heavenly beauty, were fashioned of things ephemeral by a man whose entire years were dedicated, in his own productive manner, to bringing joy and song to the lips and hearts of all mankind; indeed a noble purpose.

I myself, Most Reverend Father, have dedicated all of my years to the work of Christ. The thread of life has worn bare and my hour is approaching.

I beseech you to release Tarisio from the bonds of apprenticeship so that he may complete this mission in life. Volente Deo!

In humility, I sign myself

Francesca Stradivari, Carthusian

Brother Cosimo lowered his head in prayer. "Francesca Stradivari," he murmured reverently, *"Deo Favente, conquiescat in pace. Fideli certa merces."* For his young guest, he translated: "With God's favor, may she rest in peace. The reward of the faithful is certain."

He handed Tarisio a violin Sister Francesca had brought with her years ago, one of her grandfather's creations, which, even before she had interviewed Tarisio, she had decided to give him. He patted Tarisio on the shoulder and said good-bye.

Moments later, the tall, angular youth, chin high, walked proudly out of Saint Sigismondo, crossed the courtyard littered with the mementoes of last night's festival, and was off on the dusty highway toward Milan and home. The warm Italian sun smiled down upon him.

*View of Milan showing cathedral*

*A street in Milan*

# CHAPTER 6

THE TARISIOS LIVED in a third-floor apartment in the Piazza del Tressano, almost within the shadows of the Palazzo della Ragione, by 1809 only a dismal reminder of the city's medieval glory. Not too far away towered the outstretched marble fingers of the Duomo, Milan's great cathedral, resplendent in its rocklike beauty.

Although it was now late in September, Milan was still hot and dusty. The Tarisio apartment was overcrowded, for in addition to Luigi's father and mother, his sister lived there with her husband and infant son.

Less than a week after his visit to Cremona and Saint Sigismondo, Tarisio was back home with the beautiful violin Sister Francesca had given him. He did not know the exact moment when the decision to hunt the lost violins of Cremona had crystallized in his mind, but it had been sometime during the long hike home.

He told his father of his plan. He would travel throughout the country on foot, hunting these violins. He would play for dances and do carpentry for his keep. Then, after he had found the violins, he would take them to Paris, where they were appreciated. Someday, he told his father, he hoped to be wealthy and respected. Meanwhile, he had an important letter to the Bishop, releasing him from his apprenticeship.

Tarisio's father was greatly impressed with Sister Francesca's letter, but sad as he handed it back. There would be no violin-collecting career for Luigi, nor would there be the life of a carpenter. Milan was at war, and that very morning the police had brought notice of Luigi's conscription.

So Luigi Tarisio, his ambition thwarted, went away with the army, a seventeen-year-old boy to whom every day that stood between him and his dreams seemed like an eternity. He fought against both the French and the Austrians, at Lodi, Piacenza, Casalmaggiore, Guastalla, and Mirandola. At Mirandola grapeshot wounded him in a leg, and then the fighting was over.

He was in his middle twenties, and at loose ends. Often during the war he had thought of Sister Francesca and his visit to Cremona. There still was the notion in his mind that he could hunt old violins and sell them, but his immediate need was a livelihood, and the only trade he knew was carpentry. However, his own Strad was in Milan, and the thought of carpentering for the rest of his days disturbed him.

One day while en route to his home in Milan, Tarisio encountered a farmer in a village who needed repairs to his house. He undertook the work, and while engaged in these labors found an old violin case containing an Amati. Some of the glue had dried out and the fingerboard was loose. It also lacked pegs; the bridge was missing, and the remaining strings were frayed to uselessness. But it was a beautiful Amati, and Tarisio was so delighted that the farmer gave it to him on the spot. In its condition, it seemed worthless, and although it had been in the family for many years there was no sentiment attached to it as far as the farmer was concerned. Tarisio learned then that farmers had sentiment for nothing that could not earn its own keep.

Perhaps that moment was the real start of Tarisio's quest. When he returned to Milan six months after the war was over, he had picked up another half dozen old violins, and out of curiosity he had stopped to visit present-day violinmakers in cities wherever he chanced to be. He found in these men what he felt was a curious attitude toward the old Cremona makers. He had met makers like Joannes Franciscus Pressenda in Turin, Joannes Gagliano in Naples, and Pietro Pallatta in Perugia. And there had been Ceruti in Cremona, Soliani in Modena, and others. They all gave Tarisio the impression that they thought there were no violins which could be compared to their own. Some ridiculed Guarneri and called his work clumsy. Others attempted to belittle Stradivari and declared that because he had made so many violins they were valueless. They believed that nothing made in large quantities could have good quality. Tarisio would listen and go away without arguing the point, because, without really knowing why, he knew they were wrong and the fact that he knew it was enough to satisfy him. Besides, he reasoned, it was good that Italy felt that way—good for him—for so long as Cremona violins were considered of little value his quest would be an easy one.

After a joyful reunion with his parents, whom he loved dearly, Tarisio settled down to his old trade. He needed to accumulate money for further travel. In his spare time he repaired his fiddles.

One day, irked by the regularity and responsibilities of family life after many months of carefree vagabonding, and anxious to begin his search, Tarisio decided to go to Mantua to see Joseph Dall'Aglio, a violinmaker whom the family had known in the past. He also wondered if the violins Sister Francesca had mentioned were still there. Mantua was about 120 kilometers from Milan, but this was nothing to a man who knew distances as he did, and not so far when one is not in a hurry. Indeed, in the summertime it was a pleasant journey.

So one fine day he took off on foot, mindful of his destination, but ever fascinated by a countryside at peace. To Tarisio the province of Lombardy was the most beautiful place in the world, but hard to see; not like Tuscany, where one constantly passes from the mountains to the plains and back again. Lombardy was different. The roads were endless and the cities far apart, and, more often than not, they were just market towns. But there were green meadows and quiet, placid lagoons; and at night the white oxen gathered in the streets, drawing their filled carts to the winepress, and leaving an aroma that delighted Tarisio.

He found six Stradivari violins the day he reached Mantua, in addition to the Guarneri he was to take on his first trip to Paris. The fabled Italian city left a lasting impression upon him because he found it so different from what he had expected. In his mind was the same picture later painted by Charles Dickens:

> . . . was the way to Mantua as beautiful when Romeo was banished thither, I wonder? Did it wind through pasture land as green, bright with the same gleaming streams, and dotted with fresh clumps of graceful trees?
> Those purple mountains lay on the horizon then for cer-

tain; and the dresses of these peasant girls, who wear a great knobbed silver pin through their hair behind, can hardly be much changed. Mantua itself must have broken on him in the prospect, with its towers and walls and water. . . .

But this was only a mirage, for Tarisio found a stagnant city, sad and forlorn, decaying in the dampness of its own lagoons. For him the name Mantua had conjured up the vision of a cool caress on a blazing afternoon, a place of beauty and languor. But the Mantua Tarisio saw was a city of dirty, narrow streets and somber squares, lonely, and corroded by time. The fine old buildings had fallen into ruins and leaned awry. Even under the lenient Austrians the people appeared to slink about apprehensively, and mosquitoes, bugs, and flies seemed to have taken over the city.

The Piazza dell'Erbe was still beautiful, but one had to beware and walk lightly, for all beneath was rotten. On that square Tarisio found Dall'Aglio's shop. Dall'Aglio was working and they talked about violins. If Tarisio wanted Cremonas, the violinmaker told him, he should go to the Corte Reale and find the caretaker, who would give him all the Stradivaris he could carry away. Tarisio recalled then that Sister Francesca had told him the same thing.

If the depression of Mantua had surprised him, this was nothing compared to what he found when he reached the Corte Reale, ancestral home of the proud Gonzagas. Of its past glory almost nothing was left. There was an aura of decay about the place. The windows no longer shut, and it was hazardous to stand beneath a cornice for it might come tumbling down upon one's head.

Tarisio found the caretaker in a little suite of rooms in the rear. A priest from the church of San Andrea, he guarded the magnificent ruins. He offered Tarisio food and rest. Tarisio took out his violin and played a simple but merry tune so that even the dust seemed to dance. Then the priest played Tarisio's fiddle. After a while he disappeared and finally returned with six wooden boxes, each containing a Stradivari in sad disrepair. The exchange was quickly made. For a cheap, shiny fiddle Tarisio got six Strads. It was that easy; all the priest was interested in was one violin that he could play on, to while away his lonely hours.

Then and there Tarisio vowed to himself that the priests of San Andrea would someday receive a handsome gift from him. There was no thought in his mind that he might be robbing the church of these treasures. And no one ever accused him of it, for there was something about Luigi Tarisio that said, more clearly than words, that he and old fiddles simply went together. As time went on, and he continued to ransack the untouched storehouse of Italy, this fact came to be accepted wherever he went. Soon he possessed a dozen fine instruments, then two dozen; and there came a day when he had so many that it was time to go to Paris to sell some.

So he picked out ten of his best, and towards the spring of 1827 he headed for Paris on foot.

*Map of Mantua, about 1700*

*Jean Baptiste Vuillaume*

# CHAPTER 7

D AWN INTERRUPTED Tarisio's story. First the bright rays
of the sun stabbed at the draperies in the room where
Vuillaume, thrilled beyond words, had been listening to
his guest's story. Then the shrill awakening of a nearby
marketplace rent the air.

The Frenchman shook the cramps out of his legs and
led Tarisio to a French window opening on a patio. He
opened the curtains and the two of them looked out at
the sleeping city, its edges lost in swirling fog that curled
around the rooftops and gave the cobblestone street below them an air of unreality.

The sun was changing its color from red to glowing
gold, transforming the mist into fragments of lace that
lingered momentarily and then vanished. A few gas lamps
glowed, and an occasional oxcart rumbled by. Tarisio saw
a gendarme standing at the corner. Over everything lay
an air of somnolence and a fragrance of lilacs.

"Out there," said Vuillaume, "you will find your reward.
But come now, we have to rest. I will send word to Paga-

nini, who is now in the city, that I have finally found the violin he wants."

He stepped back inside and tugged on a cord, and as Tarisio followed a servant to his bedroom, Vuillaume penned a quick note to the famed violinist Nicolo Paganini:

My dear Maestro,
   I have just come into possession of the most beautiful violin I have ever seen, a Joseph Guarneri; the very one you have been searching for. Will three this afternoon at my salon be convenient for you to see it?

He called his servant and gave him detailed instructions for the note's delivery. Then he retired, but sleep did not come quickly. He lay with his eyes shut, and through his mind raced the story Tarisio had told him. He realized how privileged he had been, for it was the first time anyone then living had ever heard details of the lives of the Stradivari family. Years later Vuillaume was to tell François J. Fetis, Chapelmaster to the King of the Belgians and Director of the Conservatory of Music at Brussels, and also a music biographer of note, that the hours he had sat listening to the Italian had been the most enthralling of his life. The vision of Sister Francesca which Tarisio had evoked was still before him, so vividly had the Italian described her. How wonderful this nun must have been, Vuillaume thought drowsily, to have imbued his guest with such unswerving purpose!

In the next room, the joy of accomplishment upon his features, the bundle of money realized from his sale that day beneath his pillow, Tarisio slept peacefully. Hours later he was awakened by the aroma of sliced smoked pork and coffee. He was moved by his host's attentiveness. "What a delightful way to be awakened," he thought.

He dressed quickly, noting approvingly in the mirror the cut of his new clothing. Then, pleased with himself, he walked down the stairs. His nose led him to the room where Vuillaume was reading a newspaper. "Anything about me?" he asked jestingly.

Vuillaume nodded. "Aldric would never miss an opportunity like this. Sit down, I'll read the article."

Surely Vuillaume was joking, Tarisio thought. What newspaper would write about him? Vuillaume, peering over the top of his gold-rimmed pince-nez, cleared his throat and began to read:

MUSICAL SENSATION. M. ALDRIC BUYS
SIX STRADS FROM ITINERANT ITALIAN;
FOUR MORE CREMONAS TAKEN BY OTHER
PARIS DEALERS; WHO IS LUIGI TARISIO?

"That's the headline," Vuillaume explained. "And now for the rest of it.

Yesterday morning, according to the luthier M. Aldric, connoisseur of rare violins, basses, and other instruments, a ragged Italian from Milan who calls himself Luigi Tarisio appeared without appointment at his salon, carrying ten of the finest Cremona instruments he had ever set his eyes upon.

This was the first time in almost a hundred years, M. Aldric reports, that so many of the rare Cremona violins have ever appeared at one time.

After satisfying himself that the man was not——

Vuillaume stopped reading and looked hesitatingly at his guest. Tarisio's face was expressionless. "Go on," he urged. "What else?"

"This is terrible," Vuillaume said. "Absolutely terrible."

"Go on."

Vuillaume cleared his throat again, the pince-nez dancing on the bridge of his nose. His face reddened as he continued to read.

> After satisfying himself that the man was not a thief—he had dispatched a clerk to the Prefecture of Police to come and discreetly look his visitor over—Aldric proceeded to dicker with the Italian. The Italian, however, drove such a hard bargain that Aldric was compelled to call in other dealers to help finance the purchase.
>
> Georges Chanot, Charles François Gand, and Jean Baptiste Vuillaume, the copyist, were summoned, and after pronouncing the rare violins to be absolutely genuine, bought the collection for a reported 100,000 francs.

Tarisio leaped to his feet in a rage.

"Calm yourself, my friend," said Vuillaume. "Here—drink the coffee. Aldric is known for this sort of thing. Let me read the rest. It will soothe your feelings." He read on:

> M. Aldric further stated that a condition of the sale by Tarisio was that he see that these violins reach the hands of deserving young artists. He will do this at once, M. Aldric says.
>
> Research reveals that these Cremona violins—especially the Stradivaris—have hitherto been unknown on the continent. There are only a few of these famous instruments now listed in musical registers, and all of them are in the hands of royalty. The appearance of these instruments further confirms the belief that the genius of Cremona made hundreds of violins, and it is hoped that Tarisio may bring more to Paris, for the fruits of Cremona have been lost to the world for too many decades.

The men finished their meal and sipped coffee. A servant opened a box of extremely rare Turkish cigarettes. Tarisio lighted one and inhaled deeply, exhaling the smoke in short, angry bursts.

Vuillaume wagged an admonishing finger. "Tut, tut," he said. "After all, he slandered you, but he practically ignored me in reporting the story. Believe me, in Paris it is better to be slandered than ignored! Now I have really important news for you. I have sent word to Paganini, and you shall meet him this afternoon at three."

Then Vuillaume told his guest many things of interest. He mentioned Francis Tourte, as famous at making violin bows as Stradivari had been at making violins. Tourte, though now eighty years old, still made his bows, and Vuillaume knew him intimately. In fact, the Frenchman said, he was then engaged in some interesting experiments with Tourte. Some day he would present Tarisio to him. He told him about the work of Chanot, and Gand, and the Hart family in England, and as he talked he could see the interest in Tarisio's face.

The time sped by, and before either of the two realized it, the clock struck two. Vuillaume leaped to his feet. "We must leave," he said. "We shall scarcely arrive in time to keep our appointment, and no one keeps Paganini waiting—not even an emperor!"

*Francois Tourte*

# CHAPTER 8

VUILLAUME WAS NERVOUS during the ride to his salon at the Rue Croix du Petit Champ. He toyed with the drawcords on the barouche curtains and frequently looked out anxiously. Paganini was a temperamental devil, he said, a genius of unpredictable mood. He could handle the great man, but he was afraid Tarisio might say something to send him into a temper. Would Tarisio, as a favor, say absolutely nothing when Paganini came in? Vuillaume had his reasons. Tarisio nodded, puzzled and disappointed.

The barouche clattered on, the horses beating a monotonous tattoo on the cobblestone street. Again the Frenchman turned to Tarisio. "I believe," he began, "that your Guarneri will fetch fifteen thousand francs if Paganini likes it."

"Fifteen thousand francs?" Tarisio echoed incredulously. "A king's ransom for one violin?"

Vuillaume nodded. Paganini could well afford to pay such a sum. But the maestro was so unpredictable that the least word Tarisio might utter could easily touch off his temper and cause him to stalk right out of the shop.

The carriage stopped in front of Vuillaume's establishment and the two men hurried in. A clerk informed his
master that the great man had not yet arrived, so Vuillaume and Tarisio sat down to wait. Three o'clock came
and went. The minutes ticked on slowly. At three-thirty
Vuillaume leaped impatiently to his feet. Something must
have gone wrong.

Tarisio pointed to the window. "That face against the
glass has been staring at you for five minutes," he said.

Vuillaume wheeled around. A sharp-faced, swarthy man
with a beaklike nose, piercing black eyes, and long hair
done in ringlets that hung all the way to his shoulders,
peered through the glass. A sardonic smile was on his lips.

"Voilà," Vuillaume muttered. "It's Paganini. This is his
idea of a joke. Quick, turn your back and come with me."

He led Tarisio to the rear of the store, pretending un-
awareness of the figure outside. The tinkle of a bell announced that the door had opened. Vuillaume turned
around, bowed, and murmured: "Maestro Paganini, good
afternoon!"

The maestro barely nodded. "That violin you are boast-
ing about," he began. His voice snapped. There was
cruelty in his eyes and a rapaciousness that was almost
frightening—like that of a hawk about to pounce upon a
pigeon. Vuillaume knew these signs of ill-concealed curiosity and silently congratulated himself. He brought out
Tarisio's violin and, with all his aplomb and showmanship,
walked to the window where the sun streamed through.

Paganini took the violin, lifted it to his right ear and
plucked the strings gently, one by one. Satisfied that it
was perfectly tuned, he took one of Vuillaume's bows from
the counter and put the instrument under his chin. He
set the bow gently on the strings, and for a moment stood

motionless. Nothing moved in the room. Vuillaume and Tarisio stood like wax figures.

Paganini's nostrils flared, he wet his lips with his tongue, and suddenly the bow began to glide over the strings. Paganini played the concerto "Rondo ad un Campanello." The harmonics floated off like tiny clouds of misty spray, clear and sparkling; double stops and arpeggios of the most extraordinary difficulty flew from his fingers as if they were child's play. The long, white fingers of his left hand floated with flawless grace and dexterity, up and down the length of the fingerboard. He cast a spell over his listeners with tones that laced and interlaced until they seemed to melt into one.

Suddenly he stopped. An urchin had stuck his grimy little face in the door. Two tiny hands applauded boisterously and a shrill voice piped up: "Good, mister—you fiddle pretty well." Then he ducked out and disappeared.

Paganini was beaming. "A glorious instrument," he said. "Glorious. It has authority, it has the voice of the law. I. shall call it the Canon, because it is a law unto itself. How much?"

Vuillaume did not hesitate a second. In no way did he give the faintest warning that he was about to utter one of the most fantastic prices ever asked for a stringed instrument. "Twenty thousand francs."

But Paganini was his match. "Ten thousand, if I still like it after I play it for a few days. And now," he added, chuckling over Vuillaume's discomfiture, "I shall return to my quarters. This gorgeous creature deserves to be played."

He strode out of the door with the violin under his arm. "It is sold," Vuillaume said. "That is his way. He will play it all day and tomorrow he will send his check."

Vuillaume and Tarisio set out in the barouche to return home. There was satisfaction in Tarisio's face as they turned into the boulevard where Vuillaume lived, and stopped in front of spacious grounds, enclosed entirely by a low brick wall topped with a short wrought-iron picket fence. Yesterday Tarisio had been too excited to look at Vuillaume's lovely grounds. Now he admired the two-storied château, stables, and coach-house, and a small house for the concierge close to the outer gate. He told Vuillaume that he planned to see more of the city before leaving, and also wanted to buy some gifts. There was Clarice Dall'Aglio, daughter of the Mantua violinmaker, with whom he was in love; his mother, father, sister, her husband, and a nephew. He ticked them off on his fingers. "Six," he said. "You'll advise me what to purchase?"

Vuillaume chuckled. "We'll ask Madame Vuillaume. She has much better taste than I." The carriage went through the gate and Tarisio's breath was taken by the beauty of the lilacs, whose fragrance had made such an impression on him earlier in the day. They bloomed in all their glory—reds, yellows, blues, and pinks—in huge double clusters.

A servant handed Vuillaume a note. The Frenchman frowned as he read it.

"My friend," he told Tarisio, waving the note in the air, "I must leave you briefly." A matter of importance had arisen which he must attend to at once. A certain gentleman had purchased an instrument some time ago, and doubts as to its origin had arisen. Vuillaume was asked to come at once and examine it to settle the dispute. There was a fat fee in it, too. He asked Tarisio to make himself at home—for there was much of interest to see—and hurried down the steps. Moments later his carriage clattered down the drive and out into the boulevard.

Tarisio took his host at his word and began a leisurely examination of the premises. From the château's spacious windows he got a pleasant view of an old garden which contained small ornamental trees of a size similar to those in the Tuileries. Between the trees were many kinds of flowers in bloom, all showing evidences of care. At the end of the garden was a small, glass-paneled greenhouse. A workman was busy there and Tarisio strolled over for a closer look. Instead of an ordinary greenhouse, however, he found to his surprise what was evidently a violin workshop. Hanging on racks were numerous violins, some in the white and some varnished. On a shelf stood scores of small bottles filled with various colored liquids labeled "varnish." Brushes and other chemicals were set out on a bench.

There was an undefined false note in the scene that troubled the visitor, but it was nothing on which he could definitely put his finger. He examined the place carefully. Obviously this was a room where Vuillaume varnished his violins, but somehow Tarisio felt that it was all a front. The feeling of deception annoyed him, but, failing to find anything to support his belief, he finally walked away and went back to the house, where he delighted in Vuillaume's books, objects of art, and furnishings.

The second floor contained bedrooms, but Tarisio entered none of these. Instead, he opened a door at the end of the hall, and discovered that it led to an attic with a large skylight. The scene there surprised him. Here was almost an exact replica of what he had seen in the greenhouse, but far more fully equipped.

Violins in various stages of varnish were strung from

the rafters. At the end wall stood a long workbench, about thirty feet long, completely equipped with all the tools of violin-making—forms, clamps, glue, various pieces of ebony fittings, and parts of violins under construction. Tarisio was impressed with Vuillaume's skill. The man was clever. His work showed meticulous attention to detail. He made a mental note that Vuillaume undoubtedly was superior to any modern maker he had seen.

But where did the greenhouse fit in? Tarisio knew that Vuillaume, at that time, worked without assistants. He had seen freshly varnished instruments here in the attic—and the inconsistency of doing the same kind of work in two places was too much for him to fathom. Eventually he went back downstairs to await the arrival of his friend. He did not have to wait long. Vuillaume bounced into the room with all the vigor of a youth. "Well, did you have an interesting visit?" he asked.

Tarisio nodded, frowning.

"Ah, I see." Vuillaume smiled. "The greenhouse and the attic. You have seen both? Well, come into the drawing room. We'll have a drink and I'll tell you everything."

Vuillaume sipped at his drink, examining his guest quizzically. "One thing you will soon learn," he began, "is that in the making and selling of violins there is, of necessity, a great deal of showmanship. You yourself use showmanship unconsciously."

"Me?"

"Yes, you," Vuillaume said. "When you displayed your Cremonas to us, for instance, you took great care to let the sunlight sparkle on the varnish, and when you arranged them in Aldric's place you took great care to place them so that we would get the full effect of their beautiful backs. That's showmanship, my friend.

"Here in Paris there are scores of amateur fiddle-makers. They think my varnish is the sole secret of a good violin, so this is what I do: Every Thursday I hold open house here. I go down to the greenhouse, and varnish violins while my visitors watch. I dip into several pots, paint them, and hang them up. Then my visitors buy a bottle of varnish and hurry away, hoping, no doubt, to analyze Vuillaume's product. As soon as they have gone I hurry back to the attic and very carefully remove all of this varnish."

Tarisio's eyes were two black puzzles.

"After all, Luigi," Vuillaume explained, "one would scarcely expect a man to give away his own secrets, now, would one? Now, two of those fiddles you brought from Italy had Stradivari labels inside and yet they were not Strads. You yourself admitted that. One, I am sure, is a Bergonzi of early vintage, and the other an Amati or an early Bergonzi, apprentice vintage. How do you account for that?"

"I see your point, but I did not substitute the labels."

"Yet you knew they were false labels!"

Tarisio shrugged. "I suppose," he replied. "But we Italians do crazy things."

"Do you think Frenchmen are any different?"

Both men laughed, and Vuillaume knew then that he had averted what might have been a crisis in their relationship.

The two men chatted for hours, Vuillaume discussing his own specialty of copying Cremonas and Tarisio recounting his adventures in Italy. Madame Vuillaume finally called a halt to their reminiscing. If Tarisio planned to go shopping he had better get some rest, for shopping in Paris could be a very burdensome task.

Tarisio's last two days in Paris slipped away almost before he realized it. He bought shawls and undergarments
for his mother, a leather jacket, helmet, and gloves for his
father, dresses for his sister; but for Clarice, he bought
like a man possessed—dresses, lace mantillas, a brocaded
evening bag, jeweled comb, brush and mirror, perfume,
and a score of trinkets. Madame Vuillaume shook her head
disapprovingly at the man's lavishness, but Tarisio put her
objections aside with a strange brusqueness.

That evening, as the Vuillaumes drove Tarisio to the
stagecoach, they rode in silence.

"Shall we see you soon again?" Vuillaume asked at last.

"I'll be back—with more and more."

"We can count on seeing you again—even without violins?" Madame Vuillaume insisted.

Tarisio nodded gravely, saluted the couple, and climbed
aboard the coach. At the coachman's sharp command and
the crack of his whip, the horses lunged forward.

Vuillaume turned to his wife as they rode home. "There
goes a wonderful person," he said. "I shall pray that he
comes back soon, for I know that we are destined to be
friends all of our lives."

His wife nestled her head on his shoulder. "Jean Baptiste Vuillaume," she gently chided him, "of course Tarisio
will return. He needs you."

Tarisio settled back in his seat and looked with pleasure
at the street scenes of Paris. His seat was above the street,
at approximately the height of a tall man—a most pleasant
vantage point. One could easily see everything from here.
There was a good view of the stores, buildings, and points
of historic interest, monuments, bridges, and gardens.
Easily the largest vehicle in the streets, the coach took the

right of way, and all other traffic hastened to get out of its path.

Tarisio was on his way home, his pockets filled with cash, and new clothing on his back. He was successful and happy.

*Horse-drawn coach in Paris*

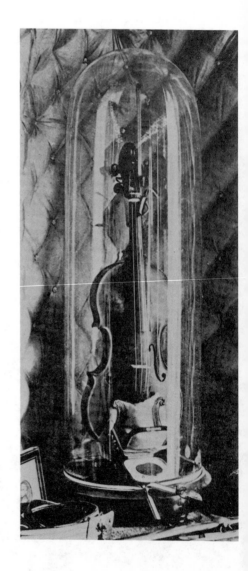

*Paganini's Guarnerius, now encased in glass in the Genoa Museum*

# CHAPTER 9

TARISIO HAD BEEN GONE a week, and musicians and lovers of the violin were still talking excitedly of the treasures he had brought to Paris. A number of notices had appeared in the newspapers. Aldric's salon, where the six Stradivaris were on display, attracted crowds daily.

One night, after a busy day during which he had seen Chanot and Gand and had discussed Tarisio, Vuillaume was relaxing at home when a loud pounding of the brass knocker disturbed the household. A servant went to the door and was quickly brushed aside by a tall, excited man who rushed into Vuillaume's parlor. It was Paganini, and Vuillaume, who knew him well, had never seen him so agitated.

"My Guarneri," Paganini shouted, "the one Tarisio brought. It has lost its voice. It croaks like a frog. It is irreparably ruined!"

He put the instrument in Vuillaume's hands. The Frenchman plucked a string and heard a dull, rasping sound. Placing the Guarneri against an ear, he plucked at all four strings, each time producing the same rasping rattle.

"What happened to your fiddle?"

"I went to London for a day," Paganini began, "and upon my return the boat docked at Boulogne. There I took a coach, and like a fool I gave my case to the driver to put away. We had no sooner started for Paris when the case fell. I opened it at once, and there being no visible signs of damage, felt somewhat easier. This evening I took out my violin to play and, *voilà*, my Guarneri had lost its voice. What can you do, M. Vuillaume?"

Vuillaume pretended to study the instrument for a long time, although the moment he had plucked the strings he had known what its illness was. But he wanted to make a copy of this violin, and knowing that Paganini would not let it out of his possession, he made the most of his chance to study it. He had some wood of first-rate quality, and very old; maple and spruce with almost identical figure and grain to that in Paganini's instrument, and in his mind was born the thought that he could duplicate Paganini's violin so exactly that not even the maestro could tell the difference. The idea so entranced him that he smiled broadly, and Paganini, mistaking the meaning of the smile, relaxed.

"You can repair it?" he asked, in the manner of one who expects an affirmative reply.

Vuillaume nodded absently, still engrossed in the copying project.

Paganini leaped to his feet. "Then fix it now," he demanded, "for I must play."

Vuillaume was startled. "Not so fast, maestro," he protested. "This is a serious repair job. One of the end blocks inside has come loose, possibly two. The belly of your violin must be removed. This is a difficult job. Then the loose end blocks must be cleaned of all the old glue, reglued, and clamped. After that the belly must be replaced."

Paganini was like a man stricken with a great grief. He vowed that he would never consent to the operation, but Vuillaume finally persuaded him. However, Paganini insisted that the operation must be performed in his own home. Although such a delicate procedure as removing the belly of a violin is best accomplished in the privacy of one's workshop without the distraction of a watcher, Vuillaume finally consented. After all, this man was Paganini, the greatest violinist of the age, and Vuillaume desired to please him. So the two went to Paganini's place.

The artist endured torture and agony as Vuillaume, using a long, flat-bladed knife, probed for a soft spot in the varnish at the point where the belly is glued to the side ribs. The blade finally found a yielding spot, and Vuillaume plunged it into the instrument. When the glue broke loose there was a crack like a shot. Paganini twisted in his chair, moaning and grimacing, uttering loud exclamations which plainly revealed the affection he had for his violin. Finally, like a surgeon proudly dangling an appendix he has just removed, Vuillaume lifted the top free, and there was not a crack in it. Paganini, bathed in perspiration, sagged in his chair, overcome with nervous exhaustion. The dreadful, nerve-wracking task was complete. Vuillaume displayed the cause of the violin's illness—one end block completely loosened, and another partly loosened.

These repairs, Paganini realized, could be accomplished nowhere but in Vuillaume's own shop. So he parted reluctantly with his instrument, but gave Vuillaume just three days to complete the work.

Several days after Vuillaume had returned the repaired instrument, Paganini met the luthier on the Boulevard, and, taking his arm, said: "I thank you, my dear friend; the Guarneri is as good as it was before. I am grateful to you and to your Tarisio for bringing it to Paris!" Then he drew from his waistcoat pocket a little red moroccan box, and said, "I have had two pins made: the one for the doctor of my body, the other for the doctor of my violin."

In the little box Vuillaume found a pin ornamented with a capital "P" formed with twenty-three diamonds. Astonished at such generosity, Vuillaume confessed: "Maestro, during the three days I had your instrument, I made a copy of it. It will be a very fine violin, and when I give it to you, even you will find it difficult to tell which is mine and which is the Cremona."

Paganini laughed derisively. "You are wonderful, M. Vuillaume—but even genius such as yours cannot duplicate the artistry of Cremona."

"We shall see," Vuillaume replied quietly.

That afternoon Vuillaume received an interesting note from Chanot, who had found a beautiful Stradivari cello top in Spain. Would Vuillaume come at his convenience to look at it? When it came to violins, any moment was convenient to Vuillaume, so, with a hasty explanation to his wife, he left for Chanot's home at the other end of Paris. He found him admiring the Bergonzi he had bought from Tarisio. It had been mounted and equipped with strings. Vuillaume noticed a thin film of rosin dust at the foot of the bridge, and knew Chanot had been playing the violin for hours.

"As good as any you make?" he asked, smiling.

Chanot gave his friend a look of pity. "As good as my fiddles? Ha! Better than all the combined skill of Vuillaume and Chanot. This Bergonzi is for Paganini."

Vuillaume shook his head. "You can forget Paganini," he admonished. "The maestro has no use for a Bergonzi. For him there is only one instrument—the big, authoritative Joseph. I repaired one for him just the other day; the one Tarisio had brought to Paris."

Chanot shrugged. It mattered little, for he knew that a rare treasure such as his Bergonzi would sell quickly. "What do you think it will fetch?"

"I'd say twenty-five hundred francs," Vuillaume said quickly. "Perhaps more from a wealthy patron."

Chanot whistled. "I thought maybe twelve hundred fifty francs—at most eighteen hundred seventy-five. But twenty-five hundred? Surely you jest!"

Vuillaume's face was sober. "You seem to forget," he said, "that this Bergonzi is one of the first to appear on the market in almost one hundred years. Tarisio told me it is one of no more than from sixty to eighty made by Bergonzi. It's rare, it's a fine instrument. It's worth money."

In the estimation of the French experts of the day, the work of Carlo Bergonzi stood next to that of the great triumvirate of Stradivari, the Amatis, and Joseph Guarneri, and Vuillaume now told Chanot the interesting facts Tarisio had related about Bergonzi.

Bergonzi was born about 1685, probably in Cremona, Tarisio had said, and was the first member of his family to make violins. His father and mother lived next door to Stradivari in the Piazza San Domenico, and it was the natural thing that he should become apprenticed to the master craftsman. As time went on and Stradivari became busier, he turned most of his repair business over to Bergonzi, his star pupil.

"But eventually the time came," Vuillaume said, "when Bergonzi was no longer content to repair violins. He wanted to make them. The pressure of the repair business, however, was so great that he could find little time to make violins. This accounted for his small output."

Bergonzi had ideas of his own, too, Vuillaume pointed out, as to what a violin should be like. He felt that the perfect instrument would combine the rich, singing tone of Stradivari with the virile sonority of the Joseph Guarneri.

"Do you think he succeeded?" Chanot asked.

Vuillaume shrugged. "Who knows what they will say of Bergonzi one hundred years from now? After all, what greater measure of a man's skill is there than the test of time itself?"

The two went over the fine points of the Bergonzi, Vuillaume pointing out the distinguishing details of the scroll, its generous size and appearance of elegance, the prominence of the "ear" or volute, the handsome wood, and the red, lustrous varnish. In the end Chanot was happier than ever with his acquisition, and Vuillaume was eager to enlist Chanot's help in cementing his friendship with Tarisio.

"We are lucky," he said, "because only the Creator could have guided Tarisio to us."

"Or the devil," Chanot replied. "You must admit that our lives will never be the same now that we are aware of this storehouse of Cremona violins! I was quite taken by Tarisio, but I wonder how he came by these instruments. Do you suppose they might be stolen?"

Vuillaume smiled. "Perhaps, in a way," he replied. "But

not as you think of it. Tarisio comes by these instruments legitimately. He pays for them—a ridiculously small price, maybe—but he pays nonetheless. In a few months he will be back with more. By the way, I have an amusing story to tell you about Paganini. Now, you have heard nearly everyone say that the reason Paganini can play staccato so marvelously is that his bow is hollow and filled with little leaden pellets which run up and down the bow when required to, and stop at once when so desired."

Chanot nodded. He, too, had heard that story.

Vuillaume had always thought this a ridiculous story, he said, but about two weeks ago, just before Tarisio's arrival, the artist had walked into his shop and taken a bow from inside his cloak. The stick was broken near the head and tied together with some string, and he had been playing with it in that condition for days. As a matter of fact, Paganini had tied it together himself. He wanted it repaired then and there, and Vuillaume saw a chance to get at the bottom of the leaden pellet story.

"I pointed to the whipping," Vuillaume said, "and asked if I could remove it. Then to the twine near the head and asked to renew that, too. Paganini simply nodded, so I picked up a knife and attacked the string near the head, as that is where the pellets were supposed to be.

"After I had removed all the wrappings, all I had was just two rough ends of a broken stick in my hand—no pellets, nothing! Paganini withered me with a look and then he called me a fool. He, too, had been aware of the story."

Chanot was smiling. "Served you right for trying to settle the issue in his presence," he commented. "But to return to Tarisio—where does he find these violins?"

It was simple, Vuillaume answered. They were in the

churches, monasteries and farmhouses, in almost every corner of Lombardy and Tuscany, lying around unplayed for years, apparently waiting only for someone like Tarisio to pick them up. And Tarisio had a way with his own people, sometimes trading a cheap fiddle in playing condition for an old, dusty Cremona, sometimes doing a little carpentry in exchange. In any case, he knew where to look.

"Perhaps we should go to Italy ourselves and hunt for Cremonas," Chanot suggested.

Vuillaume shook his head violently. "Fatal," he snorted. "All you could hope to accomplish would be to stir up greed, and price us right out in the cold. I urge you to be silent about Tarisio. But that isn't why I came here. Where is the cello top your note spoke of?"

"But what about Gand and Aldric?" Chanot insisted. "And that story in the newspaper last week?"

Vuillaume snapped his fingers. "Forget it," he advised. "Aldric will not hear from Tarisio again, and Gand is an old man. But you and I will hear from Tarisio, for he knows we are sympathetic to him, and he trusts us. Now, the cello top, please."

Chanot hurried into another room, and returned with a beautifully varnished top, which Vuillaume inspected minutely.

"No doubt about it," he said. "An excellent example by Stradivari. But where is the rest of the instrument? And why is the varnish blistered so?"

"One question at a time," Chanot said. "First of all, I do not know where the rest of the instrument is. Second, the varnish is blistered because a certain butcher left it in his window exposed to the sun all day, and it is a wonder there is any varnish left at all."

A few months earlier, Chanot continued to explain, he

had been in Madrid on business and chanced to pass the
shop of Ortego, the Spanish violinmaker. And there, in
Ortego's window, lay this cello top, crying to be rescued!
Chanot had recognized the workmanship and gorgeous
varnish at a glance. He bought it for a few francs, and
then pressed Ortego for details. The Spaniard told him
that a woman had brought a cello in, complaining of its
poor tone and asking that it be repaired. Ortego had removed Stradivari's top and installed one of his own.
Chanot, angered by the butchery of a masterpiece, had
stalked out of Ortego's place. "So here we are," he now
said. "Now, why don't you write Tarisio and tell him
about it? Perhaps on his next trip he will try to find the
rest of this cello, and if he can, Europe will have another
fine Cremona."

Vuillaume clapped his friend on the back. By all means
Tarisio should know of this, but Chanot should be the
one to write. Vuillaume already had Tarisio's friendship.
This was Chanot's chance to win it for himself.

Vuillaume took a card from his pocket and wrote:
*Signor Luigi Tarisio, Via Legnano, near the Porta Tenag-
lio, Milan, Italy.*

"I predict," Vuillaume said, "that should Tarisio find the
rest of this instrument, it will turn out to be the finest cello
Stradivari ever made. We'll call it 'the Bass of Spain.'"

Chanot laughed. "Always the showman," he remarked.
"But why the Bass of Spain? People will think you mean
the monstrosity we are beginning to see so much of these
days."

"I did not say double-bass," Vuillaume replied. "Besides I am sure you have noticed that when our French
composers score their music that they always refer to this
particular instrument as *la bass*—low down." He smiled,

patting his stomach. "Is my name not good? Does not the 'Bass of Spain' conjure up for you the vision of something in the king's own palace? And is that not good?"

"Oh, yes," Chanot replied. "That sort of thing is wonderful, and perhaps just what our art needs. I shall write to Tarisio tonight."

*Pictured above are (1) Nicolas Lupot, 1753-1824; (2) Charles Francois Gand, 1787-1845; (3) August Adolphe Gand, 1812-1866; (4) Charles Adolphe Gand, 1812-1866; (5) Charles Nicolas-Eugene Gand, 1825-1892; and (6) Gustave Bernardel, 1832-1904.*

*By the river in Paris*

*Street scene in Paris*

# CHAPTER 10

FOUR OTHER PERSONS occupied the coach with Tarisio as
it rolled out of Paris: a middle-aged man with a boy
obviously his son, and a young couple. Tarisio gave them
a cursory inspection, then turned his attention to the
scenery. The big coach was crossing a bridge over the
Seine, and the river traffic below fascinated the Italian.
Boats and vessels of many types were moving in all directions. There was a hint of approaching darkness in the
sky. Tarisio consulted his schedule, and saw that their
first stop for the night would be at Melum.

After the coach had passed the outskirts of Paris and
had begun to cut into the rural areas, Tarisio felt the first
nostalgia he had experienced since leaving Italy months
earlier. He thought of his homeland and its incomparable
beauties—the olive orchards with their oddly shaped trees,
each having an individuality of its own, their branches
of an indescribable green—warm and pleasing to the eye;
the chestnut groves with their small, shaggy trees over-
flowing with gorgeous, tassel-like blossoms. And the vineyards—ah, there was no other place like Italy with the

heady scent of the countryside, the harmonious colors, the hills and valleys, and the beauty-loving people!

The coach sped on, came to a turn in the road, screeched down a steep hill, and a few moments later stopped in front of an inn. The travelers, glad of a chance to stretch their limbs, climbed down quickly and went inside. Tarisio had no desire to spend the evening with his stagecoach companions—he would be imprisoned with them too many long hours as it was. So after a hearty meal he retired to his room, a pleasant place overlooking the main highway, and went to bed at once.

Weariness seemed to ooze from every pore as he surrendered himself to the downy mattress. How tired he had suddenly become! The thought amused him; only a few short weeks ago he had not seemed to mind the hardship of walking, or the stubble of a cornfield as a mattress. But a few nights in Vuillaume's house—and now this heavenly bed—had spoiled him. He knew that he would never again settle for less.

Muted sounds came from the inn's stable—the neighing of a horse, and the braying of a donkey. The scent of lilacs floated through the window, intermingled with the breath of sweet clover and the heavy aroma of freshly cut grass. A slight wind had come up, rustling the leaves in a loud whisper; and then the rain began to fall, each drop beating its separate note on the roof. It was pleasant there in the big bed, warmly covered, where one could drink in the fragrance of the evening, and Tarisio quickly fell asleep.

It was nearly dawn when snorting horses and the clank of metal upon metal awakened him. He listened for a moment, and then heard the deep, muffled voices of men, a sharp command, an apologetic reply. Quickly he climbed out of bed and walked softly to the window. Fifty yards away, in the bright light of the moon, Tarisio saw the inn-keeper talking and gesticulating excitedly to soldiers. The moon glinted off the metal helmets of half a dozen men whom he recognized as French troops, mounted on tall, strong horses. Tarisio knew they were French troops because he had encountered them more than once in Italy. But what were they doing abroad tonight? The war was over, the fighting finished. After a few minutes their leader raised a hand and the patrol galloped down the road. Tarisio went back to bed and slept fitfully until it was time to arise.

The coach was outside waiting when he came down, and after a hurried breakfast, the passengers climbed aboard. It was then that Tarisio learned the reason for the nocturnal disturbance. His Majesty the King, Charles X of France, took no chances of bandits raiding his subjects; and this main highway to Marseille was therefore heavily patrolled. Tarisio was relieved. After all, he carried a fortune hidden in his money belt.

It was half-past four in the morning when the coach got under way. Morning arrived in flaming light. One moment the dull, eerie haze of half-light had bathed everything in dewy fog that floated over the road and fields like thick clouds. The next moment the sun soared up over the countryside and the world was bright as noon. But Tarisio was the only one inside the coach to witness the sunrise. Every-one else was sound asleep.

A day later, when they reached Lyon, Tarisio took leave of his fellow travelers and transferred to an Italian coach. It was a far cry from the luxurious Paris-to-Marseille express. Its interior was dark, the leather seats worn, and the vehicle old and drafty. Besides that, the trip from Lyon to

Milan promised to be dull. He noticed ruefully that he was the sole passenger; on the perch in front sat a single driver, so Tarisio climbed up and took his seat beside him.

The coach rolled on across Piedmont. Everywhere Tarisio saw signs of spring-planting activity in the fields. Here and there were the scars of war, some of which he himself had helped to inflict. Several days later, the coach reached Arona, in the foothills of the Alps, and the scenery changed sharply. The rolling countryside was lush with spring's vigor. Gentle Lake Varese, azure-blue and seemingly bottomless, nestled up to the city's feet. Small waves lapped at the shore. The coach stopped long enough to rest the horses, and from their seat atop the coach, Tarisio and the driver, who by now had become friends, admired the scene.

"Look at those little swells of water," Tarisio remarked. "They run up to the shore like a small child teasing a friendly giant, brush it fleetingly, and then run away."

"So they do," the driver replied, "so they do."

Tarisio pointed to a cluster of buildings across the lake, indistinguishable at this distance, but obviously part of a settlement. That was Varese, and from there it was only fifty or sixty kilometers to Milan.

An hour later they rolled into the arcaded streets of the little village. The coach stopped, and Tarisio took his new friend to a barricaded street that ended at the edge of a precipice. As he looked out at the vista before him, the driver gasped, because this was a new route and a sight he had never seen before. There lay the plains and rolling hills of Lombardy. In the distance the Alps frowned down, and the sun, coming around the clouds, played strange tricks on the sprawling panorama.

"This is Lombardy," Tarisio said. "This is the land for

which the French, the Austrians, the Germans—yes, even the Russians—have fought. This is the land where Cremona lived and died."

Everything else in Varese was anticlimactic: the fifteen chapels which lined the steep, paved passage to La Madonna del Monte like beads on a rosary, the Sacro Monte and its shady chestnut trees, the beauty and mystery of the shrine.

In the morning, rested and eager, they resumed their journey, and even the horses seemed to know that the end was at hand. They pranced into the road as though they were starting out on their first mile. In the early afternoon the driver pulled them to a stop at the top of a steep rise in the road. Outlined against the sky, seemingly so close in the clear air that Tarisio wanted to reach out to touch them, glistened the sparkling spires of the Duomo, the symbol of Milan. The coach plunged into the city, into its teeming streets crowded with men, women, and commerce. Tarisio was home.

*Wash hung across an Italian street*

# CHAPTER 11

I N THE NARROW THOROUGHFARE where the Tarisio family
lived, one always had the feeling of walking in a deep
canyon. Overhead, the washing of hundreds of families,
hanging on lines stretched across the street, festooned
the buildings day and night, dripping continually on a
road which the sun never touched. Dampness and drab-
ness were as much a part of the scene as the dilapidated
Palazzo del Podesta, the shabby reminder of Milan's long-
vanished glory. Del Podesta stood almost in the shadow
of the three-story building where the Tarisios lived. Beyond stood the Duomo, and its marble splendor was not
enough to overcome this aura of shabbiness. But to Tarisio,
the Via del Tresseno was Milan's most beautiful thoroughfare, because it was home—the street where his father,
mother, and sister lived.

Tingling with excitement, he raced up two flights of
rickety stairs to his parents' modest third-floor quarters. The
steps creaked and groaned under his weight. An occasional
door opened as some curious resident peered into the hall.
But Tarisio ran on, oblivious of the commotion he was

causing. He threw open the door of his home and burst in shouting, "Mama! Papa! We're rich!"

The old man and his daughter were eating breakfast, while his wife hovered over the stove. For a moment, startled by Tarisio's unexpected arrival and new clothing, all three stared at him in astonishment. Then his mother padded quickly over to her tall son and clasped him in her arms. Tarisio kissed her and his sister, patted his father affectionately, and then sat on a chair which he had turned backwards and straddled, his arms akimbo on the high back.

The father looked at him gravely. "The other day," he said, "one of the carpenters told me that you had inquired about an attic in the Via Legnano near the Porta Tenaglio. You are planning to leave us, my son?"

"No, no, Papa," Tarisio cried. "That is for business only —a place to store my violins! But of that—more later. Look." He removed his coat and, opening his shirt, reached in and unbuckled his money belt. A large bundle of franc notes fluttered down on the table. The father crossed himself. Mother and daughter were speechless. Then the old woman began to cry.

Tarisio gathered his mother to him. "Now, now," he said gently. "It is honest money and all for us. Thirty thousand francs!"

"You got all this for those old violins?" his father asked incredulously. "Why, just the other day I saw one at the place they call Chiaravalle, where I am doing some repairs!"

"Later, Papa, later," Tarisio interrupted. "Listen, we have all this money. I know a little farm at Fontanetto— just a few hours' ride from here—and I can buy it for fifteen thousand francs. Let us all go and look at it."

It was a great day for the Tarisio family. Luigi told them his story, describing the hardships of his walk to Paris, his reception at Aldric's salon, his visit with Vuillaume, and his trip back. The joy in his father's face as he told of meeting Paganini was reward enough. The elder Tarisio knew nothing of music, but, like nearly every Italian, he venerated the maestro.

The Tarisios arrived in Fontanetto early that afternoon and fell in love with the farmhouse. The rooms were spacious. Mother and daughter were impressed by the kitchen and sleeping facilities. Luigi quickly made all financial arrangements, and the family started back to Milan to prepare for the move. On the return trip the elder Tarisio wanted to know more about the place in the Via Legnano.

"Well, Papa," the son replied, "as I told you, it is for business. I can make money finding and selling these Cremona violins, and I need a place to keep and repair them when necessary."

"But why can't you do that at the farm? It is a much nicer place. The Via Legnano no longer is a desirable neighborhood, you know."

Tarisio explained. He had to have a place in the city because he would be getting mail, and delivery was much more certain and faster there than in the country. There were other reasons, too. He would be traveling a lot, all around Milan, and the city quarters would be much more convenient. Besides that there was his brother-in-law Giuseppe, whom he despised. By maintaining separate quarters he could keep family irritation at a minimum. The reasons seemed to satisfy his father.

After a while the mother stole a shy glance at her son,

and ventured: "I noticed some packages at home that you
didn't open. A young lady perhaps?"

Tarisio blushed. "Now, Mama," he said sheepishly. "You
know there is Clarice Dall'Aglio. I brought her some
things from Paris. As soon as we move, perhaps the day
after tomorrow, I will go to Mantua and see her."

The elder Tarisio peered at his son. "Don't get too ex-
excited about that girl," he said worriedly. "I've been hearing things about her. You know this job I have been
working on at Chiaravalle? Well, there is a fellow there
who comes from Mantua. When I found that out it was
natural for me to inquire about the Dall'Aglios. The old
man is still making fiddles, and Clarice is now a beautiful
young woman and plans to get married."

"But that is impossible," Tarisio cried. "She was always
promised to me!"

"But you have been away a long time, my boy," the
father said. "And if she is half as beautiful as this carpenter
says she is—well, somebody was bound to grab her.
Maybe, as Mama says, it is only idle gossip."

"I'm going to Mantua tomorrow," Tarisio snapped.
"Giuseppe can help you move."

The parents looked at each other knowingly, and with
heavy hearts, for they had not told Luigi everything.
They knew that the girl he had always been in love with
already had set the date for her wedding to the other man.

After depositing his parents and sister in Milan Tarisio
left to attend to other things. He had much to do and
there was business which could not wait.

Milan had changed during his absence. The city seemed
gayer and the people happier. Tarisio sensed the change,
but could not determine its cause. The traffic was the
same as he had always known it. Horsedrawn trolley cars

lumbered noisily along crudely connected tracks, and there were the familiar drays. Elegant ladies strolled on the sidewalk, protecting their heads from the bright sun with dainty parasols. Here and there a storekeeper watched the passing throngs from his doorway. Window washers on great ladders removed the grime from windows high above the street. Tarisio saw a familiar fruit stand and waved at the proprietor. It was then that he realized the change that had come over Milan. There were no French troops, nowhere the colors of France, nowhere the rhythmic tramp of feet, the clang of metal, the obsequiousness of awed people who wait respectfully while soldiers pass. What a difference it made! No wonder Milan was happy; Tarisio, too, found himself smiling.

He crossed over from the shady side of the street and walked rapidly on. After a while he turned into an alley to an establishment where he could buy an old buggy and horse. He found what he wanted and drove away, feeling very much the equal of Vuillaume with his fancy French equipment.

For the moment, what his father had told him of Clarice's interest in another man had vanished into the background of his thoughts. Sitting in the driver's seat, he felt like a conquering hero, for it mattered little to him that the buggy was dilapidated and in need of paint, or that the horse seemed old and resentful. They were his to command. How different this would make things, he mused. The trip to Chiaravalle to see the violin his father had mentioned would be nothing now. Before, when he had walked on these fiddle-hunting expeditions, the few kilometers to Chiaravalle would have taken up the better part of a day. With a horse it was only a few hours.

He could go to Pavia—to the Certosa, where there were

old fiddles. There were Carthusians there too, and his thoughts wandered back to Sister Francesca. He would get along with Carthusians, he reflected. Behind the gingerbread façade of the Certosa were violins, because many years earlier a fine orchestra had played there. The church would be a good hunting ground for Cremonas.

A few kilometers north of Milan was the village of Monza, famous in Italian history for centuries. Tarisio knew about Monza. This was where, in ancient times, the emperors-elect were crowned kings with the "*Iron Cross of Lombardy*," which Tarisio himself had often seen preserved high over the altar of the Duomo in Milan. Tarisio knew the Lambro River, which flowed through the heart of the village, and he knew the Basilica of St. John the Baptist. There were Cremona violins in Monza, too.

In the opposite direction lay Bergamo, a city that crouched upon a series of hills. Bergamo is girdled by ancient walls above which her towers thrust, and in the background are the mountains, their bulky shoulders, capped with white, squared against the horizon. There, he knew, were San Allessandro in Colonna, San Bartolomeo, San Spirito, San Bernardino, and San Allessandro della Croce; all miserable and poor. Cremonas there? Of course, Tarisio thought; for there was a time, far back, when the violins had sung in these churches too. Perhaps he, with his French francs, could remove some of that gloom —in exchange for violins, of course.

He would go again to Brescia, where he once had been as a soldier, to Verona, Modena, Parma—perhaps even all the way to Genoa and Turin.

He eyed his horse with new interest. Would the beast make it? Tarisio decided that it could. He slapped the reins against the horse's rump and the animal quickened his pace. Soon Tarisio turned into the Via Legnano, and pulled up in front of a dilapidated two-story building. The first floor contained a restaurant. The second floor was vacant, he knew, but his attention was focused on an outside stairway that wound around the side of the building and led to an attic. This would become his "business office." This weatherbeaten building, crying for fresh paint and nails, in time would become a storehouse of the world's finest art, the poor man's Louvre. The idea made Tarisio smile as he entered the restaurant.

The man behind the counter, who was the proprietor, cook, and waiter, eyed him dourly. "You back again?" he asked, in the manner of a man who wished it weren't so.

"I am not a ghost," Tarisio replied.

The proprietor's eyes ran up and down Tarisio's figure, taking in the stylishly cut French suit, the quality and fit, and the sleek black shoes.

Tarisio quickly guessed the man's thoughts. "I understand," he said. "You think I am dealing in some kind of contraband?"

He drew a hundred-franc note from his pocket and slapped it on the counter. "I am an honest man," he growled. "I am a carpenter and a bit of a musician. I happened to have some good fortune. That is all. Here is the rent for six months."

"When do you move in?"

"Now, at once."

They argued a while. Tarisio had seen the place before leaving for Paris and had asked that it be held for him, and the owner wanted to be paid for the months the place had been vacant; but Tarisio refused, and in the end had his own way.

He was pleased with the attic. The rafters were enclosed, and the rooms were compact and tidy. An oil lamp hung from the ceiling. He lighted it, and then inspected his new quarters. The place was not elegant but it would be the most comfortable home of his own that he had ever known. There was a single bed against one wall, a coal heater at another, and a hooked rug on the floor. Other articles of furniture included a tall chest of drawers, and an easy chair that was old and frayed, but quite comfortable. At the other end of the attic was a bathtub and washstand.

Tarisio walked into his parlor and stretched himself comfortably in the easy chair. Soon, he told himself, the place would be bulging with Cremonas. The thought pleased him and he sat for a long time, daydreaming of things to come. Then he remembered a letter the landlord had handed him. Turning it over he saw the inked imprint of Chanot. He opened it and started to read.

Dear Tarisio,

I send you greetings and news which I trust will be of interest. Some time ago, when I was in Madrid on business, I found the mutilated top of a Stradivari cello in the window of a Spanish violinmaker, Ortego.

Upon making inquiry I learned that he had rebuilt one of the master's cellos for a Spanish woman who had been quite dissatisfied with the original instrument. Ortego told me that while this instrument was wonderfully carved, the tone had been thick and muddy, and that by his repairs he had given it an excellent voice.

I induced him to part with the top, and upon examining it closely at home I discovered that all that was wrong was that the bass-bar had become loose. A dab of glue would have remedied the situation. This, without a doubt, must have been one of Stradivari's finest cellos. You are the man to find the rest of the instrument, and I shall gladly sell you the top and be quite content with a small share of the proceeds.

I trust that you had a pleasant journey and shall await your next visit to Paris.

M. Vuillaume sends you his warmest regards.

Ever your friend,
Chanot, Paris, 1827 A.D.

Tarisio folded the letter with a pleased smile. Vuillaume and Chanot—how fortunate he was to have met them! Already they were looking after his interests.

Suddenly Clarice intruded into his thoughts and a frown creased his forehead. Had his father really given him the facts about Clarice and her new love? Was there really another man? Was it serious? Had Clarice ever really loved him? Pangs of jealousy gripped him. In his imagination he could see her in the arms of another man, responding to his kisses. The thought drove him wild, and he leaped to his feet in a rage. At that second, had both Clarice and her lover been at hand, Tarisio could have killed them without a question.

In a moment he realized the trick his imagination had played upon him and sank limply back into his chair. He knew that anger was no way to solve this crisis. In the morning he would drive to Mantua, call on the Dall'-Aglios and see Clarice, as if he knew nothing. He would not even let on when he presented his gifts. Then, if she told him herself, he would be magnanimous and go away. That was the way to handle a situation such as this, he felt, by being kind, gentle, and understanding.

It was time to return to Fontanetto for dinner. Mama would have done her best for him. Papa, now the lord and master of an estate, would be sitting expansively at the table, full of advice, wisdom, and knowledge of how to run a farm. His sister, demure and pretty, would watch him with tender love in her eyes. And Giuseppe? Even he would be polite and deferential, and they would get along despite their differences. He and Giuseppe might even be friends, Tarisio thought. Then he laughed. He and Giuseppe friends? He, Luigi, friends with that pig? He realized anew how much he actually disliked his brother-in-law, but for love of his family he decided to tolerate the man. The reason for his dislike was simple. Giuseppe, a shiftless man with no idea of the worth of Tarisio's treasures, once had tried to use a fiddle for firewood, and Tarisio had caught him in the act.

Dinner that night was everything Luigi had expected. Mama had outdone herself, and Papa, in rare form, spoke fondly to his only son.

"Tell me about this violin business," the elder Tarisio urged. "What makes them so valuable, and if they are valuable in France and England, why not in Italy?"

"I don't know how to explain this, Papa," Tarisio began. "It is difficult to understand, and I am not sure I really know. Take the church of St. Ambrose in Milan, for instance. A rare treasure, an ancient edifice, one of our most beautiful and revered places. Where the beautiful *baldacchino* is located, there is a *palliotto* of gold and silver which encloses the altar, and which itself is enclosed in a steel case. This is locked with twelve keys, two for each door. Have you ever seen it?"

The father shook his head.

"I'll tell you why," Tarisio went on. "This *palliotto* was made more than one thousand years ago by the goldsmith Vuolvino. The front of this exquisite casket is of pure, solid gold. It covers the entire front of the altar and is held in a frame of pure silver, adorned with precious jewels and enamels. The people of Milan never go to see this exquisite creation, but the foreigners come to Milan and they pay ten lire just for a glimpse."

"This is not quite clear to me yet," the elder Tarisio remarked. "What do the treasures of St. Ambrose have to do with Cremona violins?"

Tarisio smiled indulgently. "Papa," he said patiently, "in the first place few Italians play the violin. There is only Paganini. He is the only truly great violinist Italy has. Now, Stradivari has been dead these hundred years, and so have all the other violinmakers from Cremona. There are new violinmakers today, and they laugh at Cremona fiddles as inferior. They say that they have greater skill and that their instruments are far superior. As a result, people who play today buy the modern violins. Therefore, the old Cremonas still around are valueless here. But in France and England—that is a different story. There they appreciate these Cremona violins. They are in demand. Besides, in France, England, Belgium—yes, even in Germany—there are many violin virtuosos."

Understanding dawned in the father's face.

"I see," he replied. "You are saving an art from extinction."

The old man arose, threw his arms around the son, and embraced him warmly. "I am proud of you, Luigi," he said. "May the Lord bless you."

Mother Tarisio beamed her approval. "You see," she said to all in general, "I always said my Luigi was a good boy. I always said it. And now I know."

Guiseppe, who had sat silently up to this point, cleared his throat. "This sounds like a good thing, Luigi," he remarked. "I shall keep my eyes open for any old violins."

"Thank you," Tarisio said politely. "I am sure you will not regret it."

Tarisio undressed and stretched out on his bed, which was much too short for a man of his height. His feet hung over the end, and he realized ruefully how accustomed to luxury he had become in these last few months. Only a scant month ago a farmer's haymow, reeking of the fresh excrement of cows and horses, had seemed like heaven to him. And on that long walk to Paris there had been many nights when his bed had been no more than the soft, newly tilled rows between grape vines, with a mound of earth for a pillow and all the crawling things of the night for bedfellows. He had thought that to be not so bad. But here he was, suddenly uncomfortable in his own bed, a real bed tenderly made up by his mother's loving hands, with good feather pillows and a goosefeather mattress. Perhaps it was a little short; but that, he admonished himself, wouldn't hurt him. Anyway, he reflected, the years of self-denial and poverty were at an end. He had money now, and he knew he was destined to earn much more.

He lay there, his arms folded behind his head, staring pensively at the ceiling. He estimated that he would allow himself three days for the trip to Mantua, traveling by way of Lodi. It was slightly out of the way, but the roads were better. Then he would go to Crema, Cremona, and Mantua. He would spend an afternoon and night in Crema —there might be business for him there—and then a day and night in Cremona, reaching Mantua late on the third day. That would be leisurely travel, sparing his horse and rickety buggy.

At Cremona he intended to visit his old acquaintance, Carlo Bergonzi, 2nd. The old man had taken quite a liking to him when he had seen him a few years earlier, and the time was right, he felt, to renew this acquaintance. Although only a second-rate violinmaker himself, the old man, nearing eighty, still bore an illustrious name.

After he finished in Cremona, Tarisio would ride into Mantua. The main problem, as he saw it at the moment, was whether to ride triumphantly to the Dall'Aglio premises, resplendent in his new Parisian clothes, or to wear the nondescript laborer's garb he intended to start out in. It appeared to him to be a weighty question, for he felt that Clarice would have to be impressed, and her father, too. But he did not have time to reach a decision. Sleep reached out for him abruptly, closed his eyes, and set him to snoring lustily. In a nearby room two doting old people listened. Papa Tarisio sat in his chair, a smile upon his weatherbeaten face, his ears cocked for the rhythmic sound of his son's breathing. Mama Tarisio, scarcely daring to make a sound, stood like a statue at Luigi's door, listening and watching. After a long time she tip-toed back to a chair beside her husband and eased herself down so that there would not be a single creak.

*Violin made by Carlo Bergonzi*

# CHAPTER 12

TARISIO AWAKENED EARLY the next morning and scribbled a note telling his family that he would be gone for some time. He dressed stealthily and, shoes and suitcase in hand, walked softly through the living room into the kitchen. His hand had grasped the doorknob when the soft scraping of his mother's shuffling walk stopped him.

"I have been watching you," she whispered so as not to awaken the others. "You leave without a cup of Mama's coffee and without a kiss?"

"I wrote you a note, Mama," he said lamely. "I didn't want to awaken you." Then he slid into a chair and ate the hearty breakfast which his mother quickly prepared for him.

"I will be back next week, Mama," he said. "I go to Mantua."

When he had finished he kissed the old woman fondly, and quickly left. Within half an hour, his horse fed and his buggy packed, he was rolling along the soft dirt road.

When he arrived in Crema, it seemed just as it had been some years before—somnolent and dreary, with the same people standing in the same places. But there was one difference. Before, when Tarisio had passed through, there had been activity after a fashion in the main street—white oxen, drawing carts loaded with the burgundy vintage of the countryside, had headed for the winery. It had been fall then; now it was early summer, and the street was free of traffic.

He pulled up to a livery stable and, after some wait, managed to get the owner's attention. He wanted a place for his horse, water, and food. Seeing Tarisio's dilapidated buggy and his own rough appearance, the liveryman asked for payment in advance. Tarisio counted out five francs, which the man turned over and over, curious about a currency not then widely used in Italy, but which he willingly accepted.

The two men exchanged pleasantries and Tarisio asked: "Do they need a carpenter around here, or maybe a fiddle-player for a dance? Or perhaps you know of a violin that needs repairing?"

"You are Milanese?" the stable owner asked.

Tarisio stared at him thoughtfully. "That is an odd question," he replied. "Why do you think I am Milanese?"

"Well, you are no farmer, for certain. Any farmer knows there are dances only at harvest time. So I guess you come from a large city—and Milan is the only big city anywhere near. So I ask you if you are Milanese. No offense."

"Of course," Tarisio replied. "Of course. But I do play the fiddle, and I am a carpenter."

The liveryman took Tarisio by the arm and pointed down the street to a church, next to which stood a small bell tower crowned by a lantern. "That is the Cathedral of Crema," he said.

"You mean the building with the campanile?"

"Yes. Go there and see the abbot, Father Sebastian. He may have both carpentry work and violins for you; perhaps even food and shelter for the night—if you make a good impression. If not, come back here, and I will find a place for you to sleep."

Tarisio thanked the man, patted his horse, and took his small tool box out of the buggy. A few minutes later, having walked around to the side of the cathedral, he was vigorously rapping a large iron ring against the door. He had rapped half a dozen times and was about to conclude that no one was in, when he heard footsteps on the gravel path behind him. A short, baldish, pleasant-faced priest approached, scissors in one hand and a bouquet of flowers in the other.

"You should have walked right in and made yourself comfortable," the priest said without introduction. "And eventually I should have appeared. I am quite mortal, you know, and dinner time is not too far distant." He shaded his eyes with his bouquet as he looked into the setting sun. "In about an hour, I would judge. Come in."

Tarisio followed the priest inside, and waited patiently while he performed a number of chores. First he hung the scissors on a special hook, then he filled a vase with water and, after plucking wilted petals from his flowers, put them in the vase. He sat down and motioned Tarisio to do likewise, sizing him up thoroughly, noting the case of carpenter's tools.

"And now, my friend," the priest said. "I am Father Sebastian, the abbot here, and for the next few weeks the entire staff. In other words, I am alone. And you?"

Tarisio introduced himself and explained his presence. He could do carpentry, odd repair jobs, and he could fix violins. He might even buy one if he liked it.

"No doubt you could even repair an old Cremona or two?" Father Sebastian said slyly.

Tarisio colored, and the priest raised an understanding hand. "I know," he said pleasantly. "You are really after Cremonas, and it is about time someone rounded them up. Why, just think of it—all those fine old fiddles wasting around and bringing joy to no one!"

"How do you know about Cremonas?" Tarisio asked in amazement.

The priest's blue eyes seemed to bore through him. "My son," he replied, "this church is and has been desperate for funds; I shouldn't say desperate—for the children of the Lord are never so—but we have been badly in need of money. In looking around some time ago for anything we might part with, on which we could realize funds, I ran across a number of violins. There are two Amatis, a Stradivari, a fiddle with the label of Storioni, and one by Guadagnini. So I wrote to a priest in Genoa who knows about these things, and he replied that they might fetch a little money if someone wanted them. He also said he had heard of a man in Florence who might pay as much as twenty-five francs each for the Amatis. That is how I know about Cremonas."

Tarisio mopped his forehead. Here were five Cremonas; but here, also, was a man who might drive too sharp a bargain with him. "Father," he said, beginning all over again, "let me speak with full candor."

"Pray do," the priest murmured.

"After I buy these violins—*if* I do—much remains for me to do. I must first repair them and put them in playing condition. Then I must travel all the way to Paris and England. Finally I must find someone to buy them. All this takes effort and time."

The priest got up and motioned Luigi to follow him.
They entered the church, went behind the altar, and there
the priest pointed out a group of chairs which needed repairs. He showed Tarisio a door which needed replacing,
and numerous other items calling for the skill of a carpenter.

"What do you say? Could we discuss an even exchange?
The Cremonas for your skill with hammer, nails, and saw?
Plus food tonight and in the morning, plus a night's shel-
ter?"

Tarisio examined the work, and could have kissed the
priest. He figured four hours, perhaps five, of work; a
cheap price to pay.

"When may I begin?"

"Now, or after dinner—as you like."

Tarisio ran back to the church entrance, picked up his
tool box, and within a few minutes the sound of his ham-
mering reverberated through the cathedral. Above him,
as his nimble hands went about their task, stood a huge
painting of Saint Sebastian between Saint Christopher and
Saint Roch, and Tarisio fancied that they smiled benignly
down upon him as he worked. After a while the aroma of
fresh-cooked cabbage reminded him that it was time to
stop.

He enjoyed his dinner with the priest. The abbot had
never been outside of Italy, and he plied Tarisio with
many questions about his trip, about Paris, and its people.
Finally he arose reluctantly. "Should you desire to con-
tinue your labors tonight, I can supply you with candles,"
he said.

"I am anxious to go on," Tarisio replied hesitantly, "but
what about the noise?"

"Surely," replied Father Sebastian, "to the gods who

play with thunder and lightning the sound of one little hammer is nothing! And as for those who slumber, well, into the sleep they sleep nothing created by man can intrude. Hammer away, for this labor is truly in the Lord's service."

Tarisio hammered away.

Early the next morning, after a hearty breakfast, the abbot carried in his violins and Tarisio's heart leaped when he saw them. Although none had strings or any of their mountings, all were in good condition. The Amatis were beautiful, the Stradivari not the finest of the master's work, but unmistakably genuine. He likewise was pleased with the Storioni and the Guadagnini. As he examined his find he felt that the abbot was watching him closely. Tarisio had made a bargain—the violins for the labor—and he knew it would be kept; but now his conscience troubled him. Impulsively he reached into his shirt, pulled out his money, and counted out two hundred francs.

The abbot smiled, counted off half the money and handed the change back. "I thank you for your generosity on behalf of a little crippled child," he said. "She lives near here, and there is a surgeon in Genoa who can cure her. One hundred francs will give her a new life, and for her sake I accept it."

Tarisio, humbled and sobered, walked thoughtfully out of the cathedral with his five Cremonas, loaded up his buggy, and rode slowly out of town toward Cremona. The idea of getting new lamps for old, however profitable it might seem, was good in theory only. The priest had made Tarisio uncomfortable and his conscience troubled him. In Paris these violins would bring many times what he had paid for them.

But then the memory of Sister Francesca came back to

placate him. Someday, perhaps, he could share with the church the gains of his quest, and perhaps by that time the money would be even more welcome. It was in his mind that above all, he must keep faith with himself, whatever the cost.

*Violins in need of repair*

The mysterious Stradivari viola in which Stradivari himself changed the date and which is in mint condition. The crest under the fingerboard (see facing page) has not been identified. The rarity of this instrument attests to its being valued at well in excess of $1 million (1981). Photos by Isabelle Francais.

*Inlaid viola with fingerboard removed (photo by Isabelle Francais)*

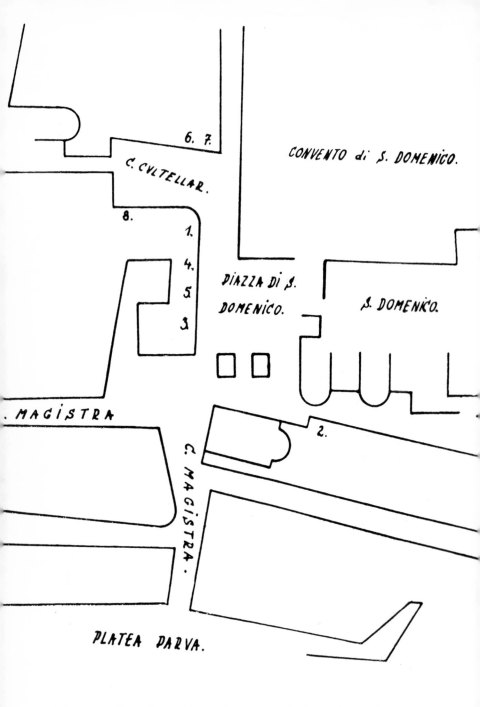

*Cremona locations of workshops: (1) Antonio and Hieronymus Amati, (2) Nicolo Amati, (3) Antonio Stradivari, (4) Joseph Guarneri del Gesu, (5) Carlo Bergonzi, (6) Lorenzo Storioni, (7) Giovanni Ceruti, and (8) Francesco Ruggeri.*

# CHAPTER 13

TIME HAD INSCRIBED its message across the features of Carlo Bergonzi with the indelible penmanship of age. Written there were frustration, lost hope, shattered dreams, and unrealized ambitions. At seventy-nine, Carlo Bergonzi 2nd, grandson and namesake of an illustrious Cremona violinmaker, was a broken old man with palsied hands and quavering voice. He had come to spend all his waking hours in a rocking chair, looking out on Cremona's main street.

People passed by all day, giving him scarcely a glance. But they also passed the home where Stradivari had worked—right next door—without a glance. It might have been that the homes of Bergonzi and Stradivari were dwarfed by some of the new beauty and grandeur of Cremona. Scarcely a stone's throw away was the beautiful Piazza del Duomo, around which were grouped the magnificent buildings which gave Cremona much of its character: the Palazzo Comunale, the Torrozzo, and Santa Maria Assunta. These bestowed upon the city the glitter of a gem sparkling in the midst of the Lombardy plain.

*Carlo Bergonzi, Cremona 1733*

*owned by Isaac Stern*

In front of Bergonzi's home, shaded from the sun by mulberry trees in bloom, two small boys rolled wine hoops in the street. Barefoot and hatless, they played a game in large squares which they had marked off by dragging a sharp-pointed stick in the dirt road.

Tarisio reined up his horse a few yards away and watched the two youngsters for some minutes, reflecting that times, indeed, had changed. When he was that age games like this were not played, for the streets then were nearly always filled with soldiers and their equipment; and, more important, children were sent out to work as soon as they were old enough to run and play.

He wondered, as he watched the excitement of the boys and listened to the shrill shrieks and laughter, whether Bergonzi would remember him. It had been ten years since he had seen the old gentleman, ten years since he had unfolded his hopes and dreams to this descendant of an old Cremona family. At that time, still in the service of the Duke of Tuscany, resplendent in the royal colors, he presented a splendid appearance. He carefully skirted the children and strode to the Bergonzi home.

Whatever fears he had that the old man would not recognize him were quickly allayed. Perched in his rocker at the front window, Bergonzi had spotted him, waved joyfully, and then snapped a command over his shoulder to someone Tarisio could not see. When he reached the door, an elderly servant woman stood there.

"I am glad you came," she whispered. "He just sits there all day with never a pleasant word. This is the first time I have seen him smile in months. He likes you. He often speaks of the nice young man with the passion for violins."

With half a dozen strides Tarisio was beside Bergonzi, gently pumping his hand.

"Still with the violins?" Bergonzi began, his eyes lighting up as he saw the affirmation in Tarisio's face. "And are you having success?"

Tarisio shrugged. "Some," he replied. "There are Cremonas—but it takes a lot of looking. But you, Signor Bergonzi—are you still making violins?"

The old man shook his head, and the lines of frustration and disappointment, which had vanished when he first saw his visitor, flowed back into his face. "My young friend," he began, "I have given up making violins. Many years ago I fancied that some of my grandfather's magic or a touch of my father's skill might have been passed on to me. But this is not so. I have finally come to realize that my years of work have been in vain. Oh, my violins are played. Modern fiddles are much in demand—no one wants a Cremona around here—and my fiddles are beautiful to look at. But the voice, the song, it is not there. When my instruments are played I hear the voice of a fishwife, not the song of an angel."

"This seems hard to believe!"

The old man reached over and patted Tarisio on the knee. "I am seventy-nine years old," he said kindly. "My time is nearly finished, but believe me, I know. I had an uncle, Zosimo, who also made violins, and he, too, said that the art of Cremona has been lost.

"I have twenty-one Cremonas here, and I have spent a lifetime studying them. I have copied their measurements to a hair, duplicated their coloring to the finest shade, but the voice is not there."

"Twenty-one Cremonas!" Tarisio exclaimed.

Bergonzi smiled. "Don't worry, my friend," he said. "You shall have them before you leave."

The old man was in an expansive mood and he en-

*Antonius Stradivarius, Cremona 1691*

*owned by Metropolitan Museum*

thralled his visitor with stories of Stradivari and his grandfather, the original Carlo Bergonzi. None of the early
Bergonzis had been interested in musical instruments, although the family always had lived next door to Stradivari.
But when Carlo Bergonzi became old enough to go to
work, Stradivari took him as an apprentice, and Bergonzi
quickly displayed an aptitude for his master's art. Even
in that day Antonio Stradivari was rich, and in time
leaned heavily upon his protégé, eventually turning over
to Bergonzi all his extensive repair business.

"Grandfather was kept so busy repairing fiddles that he
never had much time to make his own."

"I understand he only made about eighty," Tarisio said.

Bergonzi nodded. "Yes, but each was a gem. My grandfather knew Stradivari's secret."

Tarisio's eyes lighted up. The old man talked on. Stradivari, besides being possessed of remarkable talent with
the knife and varnish brush, had a marvelous faculty for
selecting the right kind of wood. This was his secret, Bergonzi said. He had heard that Stradivari often went into
the forests to choose trees for his instruments. Equipped
with a small hammer, the Cremona genius would test each
tree for its musical qualities before having it cut. The old
man was not certain of the truth of this story, but explained to Tarisio that in any case, Stradivari tested the
tonal qualities of each piece of wood before putting it into
a fiddle.

Having mastered the mysteries of acoustics, Bergonzi
went on, Stradivari knew that a good violin must combine the qualities of power, mellowness, roundness of
tone, delicacy, free vibration, and a noble and penetrating
voice. Sonorous perfection was his goal, and the wood
Stradivari used was his single most important ingredient.

The fact that all kinds of wood yield a sound had been known for a long time; in fact, in 1636, Mersenne, in his *Traite de L'Harmonie Universelle,* speaks of the sonority of wood and indicates the use of percussion for knowing and determining it. Stradivari was aware of this, Bergonzi said, and used this method to test his wood. His practice was to use maple which would give the sound of A-sharp, and pine with the sound of F.

To determine the pitch was comparatively simple, the old man continued. Stradivari would take a sample of wood cut parallel to the fibres of the wood, and fashion a small rod about twenty centimeters long and five millimeters thick. He would put the rod into vibration by holding it between his first finger and thumb and striking it a sharp blow with a piece of steel. By listening closely, Stradivari, who had a marvelous delicacy of hearing, determined the note.

"But where did this wood come from?" Tarisio pressed.

Bergonzi shrugged. "From everywhere," he replied. He told Tarisio that the master once bought a lot of broken oars from Florentine galley vessels. The Florentines used to buy maple for oars from the Turks, and the latter, traditional enemies of Florence, had sent a supply of beautifully figured maple, guessing that because of the curl in the wood the oars would crack and split when put under stress. This proved to be the case, and Stradivari thus acquired a large supply of this figured maple. It had the exact tonal qualities he desired, and he apparently used it in some of his finest instruments.

There was one violin, Bergonzi said, that undoubtedly was made of this material. It was an instrument of absolute perfection.

"Le Messie?" Tarisio asked.

*Antonius Stradivarius, Cremona 1690*

*The Stephens*

Bergonzi nodded. "Yes, Le Messie—a violin of perfection in every sense."

"Have you ever seen it?" Tarisio asked.

The old man nodded. "Many times. It hung on a wall in the house of Paolo Stradivari—the maestro's son. And here is a strange thing: Paolo Stradivari never seemed to realize what a work of perfection it was! Let me tell you a story about him. After his father died, when he was a young boy, he came across an old family Bible in the house. On the flyleaf, in Stradivari's own hand, was a list of ingredients and quantities for the varnish he used. Paolo tore out this sheet, then destroyed the Bible."

Tarisio excitedly interrupted the old man. "Then the formula for the varnish is still in existence?"

Bergonzi shook his head sadly. "It is not. For some unknown reason, a reason he took to the grave with him, Paolo destroyed the original formula. Once, when we discussed it, he said he had made a copy. But I did not believe him, because even in Paolo's time violinmakers in France, Germany, and England wanted that recipe and would have paid well to get it.

"Anyway, to get back to Le Messie, Paolo sold it and a dozen others to the Count Cozio di Salabue in Florence."

Someday, Tarisio replied, he would acquire Le Messie, but two things puzzled him: how to recognize the fabulous violin when he saw it, and how to deal with a member of a noble Italian family. This would be a matter of extreme delicacy.

The old man believed he could assist Tarisio on both points. First of all, he said, Tarisio's dealings with the Count might very well depend upon many things—the Count's disposition, the state of his finances at the moment, and the impression Luigi would make at first meeting. He knew this to be true, because his own family had had many dealings with di Salabue. However—and it was vital that Tarisio should remember this—the Count had never held the work of Stradivari in too high regard. On the contrary, he worshipped the work of the Amatis, from whom Stradivari had learned his trade. Now, if Le Messie were an Amati, neither Tarisio nor anyone else would ever get it. The Count would have it interred with him rather than part with it.

"Perhaps I can offer him an Amati and a little money?" Tarisio asked.

It was quite conceivable, Bergonzi said, that this could be the case, but it would require finesse; of that he was certain. "And as to identifying Le Messie when you see it——"

"Yes," Tarisio interrupted, "that I must know, to the minutest detail."

"I will describe it from the violinmaker's viewpoint. And you must listen carefully. Remember, Le Messie has never been played, therefore one can only guess at the voice. You have looked upon women who were pure and women who were just beautiful. No?"

Tarisio nodded, not wishing to say anything to distract the old man.

"So, when you look upon the face of purity, somehow you know it. Your eyes say something to your heart. It is the sort of feeling one has when one gazes upon the features of a sleeping infant. That will be your impression when you finally feast your eyes on Le Messie.

"Now for the actual description. Le Messie is startling to the experienced eye. The varnish is a brilliant red, and will remind you of ripe cherries or mahogany. At first

*Antonius Stradivarius, Cremona 1704*

*The Betts owned by Library of Congress*

glance it will appear to have been laid on only an hour before. No matter how long you possess this instrument, each time you see it you will always think the varnish has just been applied. At times that thought will frighten you, because you will fear that, during your absence, some fool has tampered with it. Many times I went to Paolo Stradivari's home and saw it, and each time I would swear the finish was wet. Then, as you stare at it, a hidden quality of the color manifests itself. The colors seem to become more brilliant, and the camelhair brush marks come more sharply into focus. You have an illusion of the varnish running over the sides. Actually, there isn't a lump in it, for it covers the wood as though it were part of it.

"There is exquisite beauty in the purfling and in the absolutely perfect corners, the sharp, sweeping curve of the F-holes. The black edging on the scroll has a satin hue with a look that is different from anything else you have ever laid eyes upon.

"The pegs and tailpiece are made of a naturally yellow wood. They are as hard as ebony, but with a grain that resembles mahogany. Pegs and tailpiece have beautifully carved little figures in relief."

The years seemed to melt from the old man's face as he spoke. Tarisio scarcely moved.

Bergonzi continued his description. "The back is in two parts and shows broad waves of light instead of the usual herring-ribbed marks. Nowhere has the wood been rubbed. No harsh paper or powdered stone was used in smoothing the surfaces. All of it was done with a knife, but nowhere can you find a single knife mark! This is unbelievable, but true. The materials themselves? The spruce in the top is so perfectly matched that it is fantastic, the maple so beautiful as to defy description."

Tarisio's eyes were closed.

"You can see Le Messie?" the old man asked softly.

"So clearly," whispered Tarisio, "that I can almost reach out and touch it."

"There is a little more to tell you," Bergonzi went on. "Le Messie was not the only exquisite violin that Paolo Stradivari sold to the Count that day. As a matter of fact, it was included in the sale in a very casual manner. The *pièce de résistance*, the fiddle the Count really coveted, was an Amati. When Stradivari was apprenticed to the Amati family, he was at first permitted only to rub wood smooth. Before he was taught the art of carving he was made to master the simpler things. Good wood was hard to get in those days and the Amatis would not run the risk of permitting a careless chisel to spoil any of it. So Stradivari was put to work rubbing smooth the finished pieces, and finally permitted to assemble complete violins. The Amati coveted by the Count was the very first violin Stradivari had ever assembled himself, and one which he treasured as a souvenir, despite his feelings about the master."

Tarisio asked a question. "Le Messie, you said, was never played. How do you explain that?"

Bergonzi smiled. Being a violinmaker himself, he could understand it, strange and inconsistent as it appeared to be. Generally, when a man completes a violin, he said, one of the first things the maker does is put on the strings and test it for tone. He desires to see if he has truly captured a voice. But with Le Messie it was different. Stradivari knew as soon as he had completed it, according to Bergonzi's grandfather, that it was his masterpiece, but he never got around to stringing it up. Perhaps, fascinated by the perfection of his workmanship, he feared disap-

*Antonius Stradivarius, Cremona 1708*

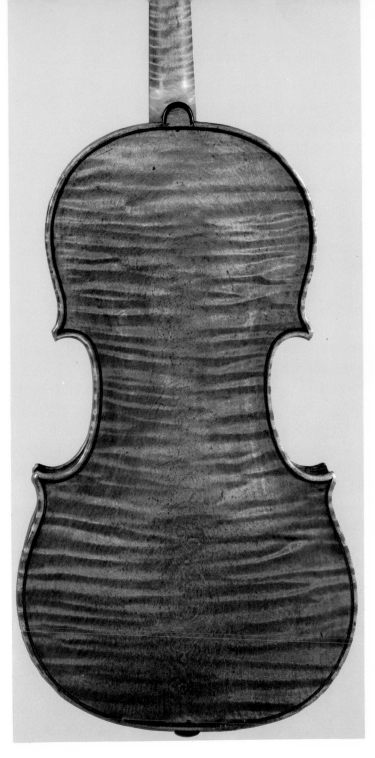

*The Soil*

pointment in the tone. Perhaps he desired to create some air of mystery about it. Who knows?

"My father used to say that at the time Stradivari made Le Messie he was turning out violins so fast that he didn't have time to play them. This particular fiddle was made in 1716, one of his busiest years. Remember, he was making violins on order from many people. I prefer to think that he was just too busy to play it and that he kept it because he had plenty of money and could afford to hang on to his masterpiece."

"This sounds logical," Tarisio said. "But I imagine such a thing of beauty would be securely kept in a safe place."

Bergonzi shrugged. "Who can say? In any case, the Count realizes that it is something out of the ordinary. The man is a fox, I know."

Bergonzi's servant brought them food and both ate heartily. Later the old man conducted his guest to his workshop, to show him his own collection of Cremonas. The studio was in the south end of the old building, a favorite exposure for violinmakers, because varnish seemed to dry best there. A skylight occupied much of the vaulted ceiling. A bar, shoulder-high, stretched from one side of the room to the other, and from this dangled numerous violins. Tarisio estimated at a glance that there were at least fifty in various stages of finish, some in the white, some partly varnished, many complete even to strings and bridge. He walked up and down the rack, examining each of the violins.

Bergonzi watched him with amusement. "Tell me," he asked provocatively, "which are the Cremonas of one hundred years ago, and which are mine?"

Tarisio stared at the display. Was the old man serious? Was he testing him? Was this a trick? Did Bergonzi really believe that one could not distinguish between the old and the new? He broke into a sweat and stepped nervously back to the rack. If old Cremonas were on this rack, Tarisio, who fancied he could spot one in the wink of an eye, had been deluding himself for years. He let his eyes rove over the violins a second time. One caught his attention. He took it down and handed it to Bergonzi. "This is an original Guadagnini," he said.

The old man nodded. "Quite distinctive, isn't it? Now— what about the rest? Which are the Cremonas and which are mine?"

Tarisio was puzzled, for suddenly he realized that he wasn't sure. It was on the tip of his tongue to say that they were all original Cremonas, but he remembered that the old man had said earlier that he only had twenty-one.

"I don't know," he stammered. "I thought at first that they were all original Cremonas."

Bergonzi nodded approvingly. "Now, examine them more minutely and then give me your opinion."

Tarisio took each fiddle down and subjected it to the most piercing scrutiny at his command. Finally, convinced that he had detected the infinitesimal differences between the original Cremonas and Bergonzi's work, he stepped back. "These are the original Cremonas," he said, indicating sixteen of the violins. "The others are all your work."

He saw confirmation in the old man's eyes.

"The likeness is incredible," Tarisio said, praising the workmanship and the color and shading of the varnish.

"But the likeness to Stradivari ends there," Bergonzi said sadly. "My violins are beautiful, but they are like creatures without a soul."

At that moment Tarisio understood the despair and frustration in the old man's face. Here stood a man who

*Antonius Stradivarius, Cremona 1727*

*The Davidoff owned by Erika Morini*

for sixty years had bent every conscious effort towards learning the secrets of old Cremona and who had, to all appearances, solved them all except one; but the omission, whatever it might have been, was the most important of all. Whatever this intangible something was, whatever the event or thing that gave the old Cremonas their heavenly voices, this was the ingredient that had eluded Bergonzi.

The old man managed a smile. "The strangest thing of all," he told Tarisio, "is that today's violins are sought by everyone. Call it a whim or mood of the times, ascribe it to ignorance, call it what you will, but that is the fact."

"The other Cremonas—you said there were twenty-one," Tarisio reminded him.

Bergonzi lead him to his workbench where Tarisio saw the answer. The remarkable likeness of Bergonzi's work to the original Cremonas no longer was a mystery. Five Cremonas, each dismantled to its component parts, lay on the bench. The old man had taken his measurements exactly, to the hair's breadth, duplicating the Cremonas in every little twist and turn.

"Where did I fail?" he asked.

"I don't think you have," Tarisio replied. There was respect in his voice. "Perhaps a century from now your violins, too, will sing like angels. Perhaps that certain ingredient that gives the old Cremona a soul is nothing more than time—the gentle touch of age, the mellowing, or ripening.

"In the late spring the grape on the vine is small, green, and tart to the taste. Yet the shape of it is flawless and the color exquisite. But in the fall, in addition to the perfection of form, it acquires an aroma and taste that delight all mankind. Now, my most revered friend, I ask you this:

what ingredient has been added to the grape, the vine, the soil, or the air around it?"

Bergonzi smiled. "Of course, of course," he said. "Time —the mellowing ingredient of time." He looked at Luigi with gratitude and great affection. "The Cremonas are yours if you wish them," he said.

Tarisio did some quick mental arithmetic. "I cannot pay you what they are worth."

Bergonzi put an arm fondly around the younger man's shoulders. "You already have paid me with your faith in my work! I am an old man; I own this house and I have a little money. The violins hanging here will more than provide for all my needs.

"Of course I know these Cremonas are worth something, but I have neither the strength nor the desire to sell them and I have no one to give them to. So take them, and through them may you reap success."

Tarisio was speechless. The gift had overwhelmed him, and he silently followed Bergonzi out of the study and back into the pleasant room where their conversation had begun. Darkness had dropped its mantle over the city. Oil lamps flickered on the street, casting beams of yellowish light.

"And now, young man," Bergonzi said, "we come to the sad part of this day, the parting. Tomorrow you go to Mantua, to the Dall'Aglio girl, yes?"

Tarisio nodded in surprise. Strange that his friend should mention Mantua and Dall'Aglio. Did he, too, know something?

"You see," Bergonzi went on, "I remembered your enthusiasm for the Dall'Aglio girl and all these years I've kept my ears open. I know Dall'Aglio. He comes here frequently for my varnish. We have discussed you on many

*Antonius Stradivarius, Cremona 1737*

*The Lord Norton owned by Chas. Libove*

occasions; that is one reason I know so much about you. But I have sad news for you. Clarice Dall'Aglio is not for you, and she will never be yours."

Tarisio sat like a man stricken.

"Clarice is betrothed, and the wedding takes place the day after tomorrow. She weds a man whom she loves deeply."

"I do not understand," Tarisio said weakly. "She promised to wait."

"I know," Bergonzi replied. "I know all about that. But, in the first place you were gone so long in the fighting, and then there were your violins."

"My violins?" Tarisio asked incredulously. "What did they have to do with it?"

"It wasn't the violins—but your passion for collecting them. Clarice felt that you would never give up this quest as long as you lived; and no woman wants to be second to a fiddle!"

In his heart Tarisio knew the old man was right. What he had said made sense. The decision which had been forming in his thoughts ever since his father had mentioned this to him, crystallized suddenly.

"I can understand," he said very slowly, "that a wife and my search for violins could never exist in harmony. No man, it appears, may so divide his loyalty."

"A sage opinion," Bergonzi commented. "A wise, mature opinion."

*Display of violins and related materials*

Andreas Guarnerius fecit Cremonæ ſi
titulo Sanctæ Tereſiæ 1695

Ioſeph Guarnerius fecit ✠
Cremonæ anno 1793 IHS

Gio Paolo Maggini in Breſcia.

Anno 1733 Carlo Bergonzi
fece in Cremona

Antonius Stradiuarius Cremonenſis
Faciebat Anno 1707

*Labels of violin makers*

# CHAPTER 14

TARISIO WAS DELIGHTED when he saw his horse the next morning. His gray coat was resplendent. Brushed and combed, the fetlocks hung like silk tassels. His mane had been closely cropped, and there was a new look of vigor and freshness to the animal. This horse was not as old as he had thought, Tarisio realized, as he climbed into his rig and headed toward Mantua, Clarice, and the news he dreaded to hear. For the first time in his life Luigi Tarisio had come to experience anxiety and a dread of knowing what tomorrow would bring. Although he was now certain about what awaited him in Mantua, he still could not bring himself to accept it.

He wondered, as his horse trotted through the countryside, what his own face mirrored. Did it reveal the trepidation in his heart, or the fact that his hot, dry breath seemed to choke him, or that there were knots in his stomach? Did his face reveal fright, worry, and despair? The battlefield was never like this! Once he had heard the frightening swish of an enemy's sabre as it flashed through the air. Then he had not been frightened; nor was he afraid when grapeshot sprayed around him, whistling past his head with only inches to spare. But now, faced with the thought of confronting a girl, he found that the mere idea caused him to tremble.

To Tarisio, Clarice was like no other woman. She had deep blue eyes, blue like the sky in spring, with large black pupils that gave one an impression of bottomless depth. Her skin was without a blemish; it was ivory in color, with a touch of pink on her cheekbones. And there was about her a bubbling, effervescent quality, sometimes subdued, more often unrestrained, but always delightfully animated. Then he thought of her smile, which was always pleasant, but never warm. That, he realized, was because she never smiled with her eyes, but with her mouth only, as though pleasure was a mechanical thing one never really felt.

Love could be burdensome, Tarisio thought, for it required a great deal of thinking and imposed a strain to which he was not accustomed. As he once told Vuillaume, he wanted to love a woman without the bother and worry that this love was causing him.

The thought of Clarice's smile had disturbed him further, and he was sorry he had turned his thoughts in that direction; for the complexities of daily existence irritated him. Tarisio was a simple person who wanted to stay that way.

A pretty young thing in a corn field, busily tying a battered straw hat to a scarecrow, stopped long enough to wave gaily as he passed. Tarisio looked at her soberly, for the temptation to stop for a pleasant hour in the sun-drenched field was strong, but he resolutely brushed it aside, unconsciously urging his horse to a slightly faster pace. He had woman trouble enough.

How would he approach his problem? Should he change into his Parisian clothing and ride up to the Dall'Aglio home in the grand manner? The last time Clarice had seen him, he had been wearing the uniform of the army, much the worse for wear. He had had no money then, and he had felt ill at ease. But now he had money. He could play the grand role, and he could almost see himself riding majestically up to the Dall'Aglios. He fancied himself tall, dark, and erect, flashing piercing glances at the curtained windows where he would see Clarice, excited and overwhelmed, watching her hero come up the walk. As he reached the door, it would slide open silently and there would be a maid, curtsying respectfully, saying that Signorina Clarice waited. Stiff as a ramrod he would go in, and Clarice, confused and unable to meet his eyes, would be waiting modestly for him to say the first word. He would stand there for a moment, look at her tenderly, and then, as a father reproving his child, take her into his arms and murmur: "It is all right, my dear."

It was a pleasant thought, but perhaps it might not work out like this. Luigi remembered the old days in Milan, before the Dall'Aglios had moved to Mantua. There had always been a certain barrier of class between his family and the Dall'Aglios, and between him and Clarice. Tarisio's father worked at his carpentry, mostly around the cathedrals and churches, often six days a week and ten to twelve hours each day. There had never been much beyond the bare necessities in his home. In addition to this, his father was an untutored man, and the Tarisios had little social life. The Dall'Aglios had always lived on a higher scale, and the difference was quite plain to see on Sundays when the families met in church. Papa Tarisio always shone like a newly bronzed coin, and his mother in her bandana and one good dress looked exactly like hundreds of other peasant women. But Dall'Aglio was always resplendent in the best suits. He wore his hat at a rakish angle, and a solid gold chain across his vest spoke, in itself, of class.

No, Tarisio could not impress Clarice with his new wealth, nor with his sudden rise to elegance and dignity. It might be better to go in humbly, hat in hand, and plead his case from the heart.

A thought, long dormant in his mind, began to take on substance. He had been in love with Clarice Dall'Aglio, and he often had told her so. But—had he just assumed that she returned this feeling? Had he made the mistake of taking her feeling for him for granted? Had he really labored so hard and so long to collect Cremona violins just to place himself on Clarice's level, or had he done so because of the love he had for these instruments, for the excitement and thrill of finding them? Strange that he should have these feelings now, he thought; that at the very gates of Mantua he should be filled with doubts, and question his own motives.

But a glance to the rear of the buggy where Bergonzi's gifts lay securely tied and packaged gave him his answer. He loved these violins; he loved the challenge of finding them, the challenge of identifying them, the thrill of Paris, of distant places and new people, and he realized for the first time that Clarice Dall'Aglio had become a thing apart. Nothing would ever shake his love for her, but the violins had become an integral part of his being. He could face the Dall'Aglios now with confidence, for his strength and security lay in the little boxes behind him. They were the mute answers to almost every dream he had ever cherished. There was no longer a choice for him between the violins and the woman he loved, if there ever had been one. The conflict within him had dissolved. As his horse trotted into Mantua, Tarisio felt as though he had become some new being, who, floating languidly in space, could look compassionately down upon the bewildered man with the reins in his hands.

Mantua had changed. Some of the deathly stillness, the feeling of rot and ruin that he had noticed on his last visit, was gone. The city was gay, and filled with Austrian civilians. This was the aftermath of the fighting, he thought, and the foreigners' presence augured well for the city for, after all, the Austrians were there to stay. He checked into the Flying Horse, quartered his horse, and decided to have a bite to eat.

It was still daylight when he came out of the restaurant and went down the street to the Dall'Aglios. The picture that greeted his eyes as he strode up the gravel walk was not at all as he had imagined. A smartly equipped horse and carriage stood outside. He heard the sounds of laughter on a side veranda and saw a number of people sitting there. Suddenly he felt shy and hesitant, but it was too late to turn back. Dall'Aglio already had spotted him and was shouting a greeting. Tarisio stepped forward and a young man who had been sitting beside Clarice stood up.

"Meet my future son-in-law," the violinmaker boomed. Tarisio realized that Dall'Aglio had been drinking, but he stuck out his hand. Then, turning to Clarice, he bent gallantly and kissed her hand.

Dall'Aglio stepped between the two young men and put an arm around each. "Luigi," he said gaily, "while you were fiddling, Angelo here was dancing." He laughed uproariously. The girl murmured a protest, and her mother led the violinmaker away, berating him soundly.

"An awkward pun," the young man said, looking Tarisio full in the eyes. "I'm sorry."

"Forget it," Tarisio replied. "After all, he's happy—it isn't every day a father sees his only daughter married."

"Thank you, Luigi." Clarice smiled, but her eyes were not smiling.

Church bells began to toll their evening vespers, and the setting sun and gathering gloom began to speckle the orchards and fields with patches of darkness. Tarisio shivered, but not from the slight breeze that floated through the trellis behind and fluttered around the strands of Clarice's shoulder-length hair. Her hands tightened around Tarisio's fists. "I wish it could have been you," she said, "but the time came when I realized that my love for you was not that of a sweetheart for her lover. I can't tell you how I feel, Luigi," she went on. "I cannot explain it. It is a strange thing—perhaps a feeling of tremendous admiration, or maybe just respect for your courage and integrity."

"And Angelo?" Tarisio asked quietly.

"I love him," the girl replied simply.

Tarisio looked at her for a long moment. Then he kissed her gently on the cheek, rose and walked into the house.

Dall'Aglio, somewhat sobered, sat sipping tea. "You still hunting those old Cremonas?" he asked.

Tarisio nodded.

"Fine, fine," the old man replied. "I have three in my shop—an original Carlo Bergonzi, a Strad, and a Guarneri. They are yours for a few francs. But tell me, Luigi, what is the matter with my violins, or any of the modern fiddles? What is this mania for old Cremonas? They show cracks—

the wear and tear of time, and there is scarcely one that doesn't need re-gluing."

Tarisio shrugged. "Some people like the new," he replied, "and others like the old. I belong in the latter class." There was no point in telling Dall'Aglio that for quality of tone, volume, and workmanship the old Cremonas were by far the best, and most desired by those who could afford to pay.

"Come tomorrow," Dall'Aglio said. "No—I will walk back with you now and you shall have them tonight."

Tarisio did not see Clarice again, for she had vanished into her room with her mother.

"I suppose," he commented, "it was because of my fiddles that I lost Clarice."

"I don't believe so, my boy," the father replied gently. "I think it was because she never really loved you."

There was no further reference to the subject as the two men walked away in the darkness. But from an upstairs window, two pairs of eyes watched their figures blend into the night, and one pair was red with tears.

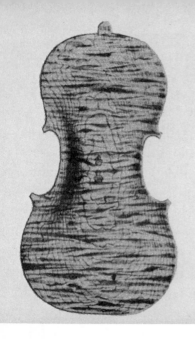

*One-piece backs, cut on the quarter (left) and cut on the slab*

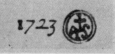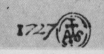

*Several of Antonio Stradivari's labels*

# CHAPTER 15

UPON HIS RETURN to Milan, Tarisio went straight to his place in the Via Legnano and, after unloading his violins and carrying them up to his attic quarters, changed his clothes. He was glad that he had been able to get back so early because it gave him time for some things he wanted to do. He had several letters to write, one to Chanot thanking him for the information on the Spanish cello, and another to Vuillaume describing the twenty-five additional Cremonas he had acquired.

Vuillaume should know about it, he thought, because that would give him time to find purchasers. Tarisio had become aware of the true value of his instruments. He had Paganini to thank for that.

He decided on a simple way of storing his precious violins. He strung a rope across the room and tied each violin separately to the line. Stepping back to admire his collection, he saw that the arrangement was almost identical with Bergonzi's. It pleased him. There was only one window in the room, a small square in the end gable. Tarisio removed a pane of glass. He wanted fresh air in this room

—not too much, but enough to keep the musty odor away. It would not do to let the room become too dry, but neither did he want it too moist. If it were too dry the glue would deteriorate, and if it were too moist the wood would swell. But with the window open, conditions in the attic seemed ideal.

He then began to examine his treasures and saw that most were in excellent condition—all except the five dismantled Cremonas which had been in Bergonzi's collection. It would take considerable time to reassemble those, so he put them aside for later consideration. Some day the market might be good enough for him to sell them as they were.

One of the Strads in particular demanded his attention. Beautifully varnished, it bore a label of 1723. The yellow varnish had depth and brilliance, and was velvety to the touch. Tarisio ran his finger tips gently over the surfaces, much in the manner of a blind man, and it came to him that there was something unusual and strange about the feel of the varnish. Two things he knew about this fiddle beyond a doubt: first, that Bergonzi had obtained it directly from Paolo Stradivari, and second, that in the years it had been in his possession, the original varnish had known nothing aside from an occasional wiping off with a dusting cloth. Yet the feeling persisted that something was amiss. He continued to slide his finger tips around the top when something about the upper right side, where the performer's hand usually rests when playing in the upper positions, arrested his attention.

He went over it again slowly and then noticed a different texture in the varnish at one spot. Elsewhere it felt smooth, like satin, but up there it was hard and brittle. He held the violin up to the lamp, muttering his displeasure over the weak rays. What he needed was daylight. He moved to the one window, drew up a chair, and began to rotate the violin from side to side. At first the varnishing seemed no different than that on any other Stradivari he had seen—with full, brilliant shading which appeared to grow in depth as he watched. Tarisio long had suspected that this feeling of depth was more than an illusion. Now he realized that it was an actuality and as he stared at the top in the sunlight, he arrived at an explanation. Many coats of varnish had gone on the instrument to give it the variety of shading. It was not, as he had once thought, simply a matter of applying the varnish thicker in some places and thinner in others; the varnish was a combination of different-colored coats, and, he believed, of different kinds of varnish.

He pinched a tiny fragment off the top with his fingernail. A flake came loose and Tarisio powdered it between his fingers. It felt familiar and he thought that he had identified it. A phrase formed on his lips—a phrase despised by old-time violinmakers: spirit varnish! Was this Stradivari's secret? Had the master maker of Cremona found a way to combine coats of pure gum varnish with coats of spirit varnish? Tarisio knew that the pure gum coats often required as much as a year between applications. He thought of Bergonzi's remark that Stradivari had been pressed to fill his orders. Was this a short cut Stradivari had used? Or was it a secret blend that gave these violins their unusual tone? Spirit varnish dried in a matter of hours, but violins so coated always had a tinny sound and good makers disdained it, preferring the resilient qualities of gum varnish.

If the master had alternated coats of gum varnish with coats of fast-drying spirit varnish, it was an achievement, he knew, because one was a solvent for the other. Tarisio decided that he must discuss this with Vuillaume the next time he went to Paris.

He continued his examination of the violin, noting its double purfling. This same type of purfling appeared in the one-piece back, only in the center of the back was an ebony inlay ornamented with clover leafs at the upper and lower ends, excellent examples of Stradivari's artistry. The wood on the back and in the ribs had been cut on the slab, the beautiful grain glowing through the transparent varnish like an illuminated engraving. The top of the violin was made of close-grained pine. The F-holes were typical of Stradivari's work—long, sweeping, and graceful. The neck resembled a swan's, and Tarisio marveled at the skill and artistry. There was as much art here as in any of the fine paintings he had seen on his travels through Italy.

He went over the rest of his accessions minutely, and concluded that his theory that Stradivari had managed somehow to blend coats of spirit varnish with gum varnish would bear further investigation. He took the dismembered instruments, wrapped each group of parts separately, and stored them in one of the drawers of the cabinet. If he could not sell them as they were, they would wait for a rainy day, after he had bought clamps, glue, blocks, and other tools to restore them. In any event he could always hand them to Chanot or Vuillaume for repairs.

The idea of being able to give Vuillaume a job, of hiring a man he felt was far superior to him, delighted Tarisio. He was changing, and he knew it. The feeling of inferiority was distasteful to him, but time and success would remedy that. He was not often moved to prayer, but the urge came to him as he surveyed his new possessions, and he knelt, alone in the shabby attic, and prayed that he, Luigi Tarisio, could pursue his career with honor, dignity, and humility.

There was a sudden flash of lightning, and the roll of thunder reverberated across the sky. In the street beside his horse and buggy a tree branch hung limply from its trunk, but his horse, nibbling at some weeds, munched placidly on, unaware that death had missed him by inches. When Tarisio went outside, he saw the proprietor staring out a window at him, and it was on the tip of his tongue to go in and ask if he had heard the thunder and seen the lightning, but he decided against it. He was in no mood to risk being sneered at. If it were not for the tree limb, torn and ripped, its shattered fibres oozing with sap, Tarisio would not have believed it. There was no question in Tarisio's heart that the Lord had heard his prayer in the attic, but he made no effort to interpret this knowledge. He had been heard, and this was enough; he knew that his treasures in the attic would be safe.

Several hours later he reined his horse to a stop on a little rise in the road, just a stone's throw from Fontanetto, and looked fondly at the large gabled house—the low, rambling stone wall in front, and the green pastures on all sides. The place had a small olive orchard and a grove of chestnut trees. Behind the house were a dozen rows of grape vines. There was activity, and Tarisio smiled. He knew his father and mother—by fall there would be food in the house, potatoes, cabbage, and a variety of vegetables. He could see a plow at work.

He pulled up to the house, jumped from his buggy, and burst into the kitchen. The sight brought an exclamation of joy to his lips. The place was transformed. Only a few short days ago the kitchen had been dingy and dusty, filled with cobwebs and debris. The fireplace beside the oven had been as previous tenants had left it long months before, filled with rancid ashes and the musty odor of partly burned wood which long since had become the resting place of rats and sparrows. There had been a little pile of dislodged brick from the chimney, broken pottery, rotting articles of wear, a partly eaten loaf of bread, green with mould and crawling with worms.

But now life and order had been restored by the tireless hands of the woman who stood over the stove, stirring a mixture of tantalizing fragrance. Tarisio gathered his mother into his arms and showered kisses upon her. She had worked wonders. The kitchen was resplendent in its scrubbed glory. Broken windows had been repaired, bricks in the chimney and broken planks in the floor replaced, a broken door repaired. There were curtains at the window, colorful little covers on the table and chairs, and canned jars of food lined a shelf.

The family reunion was complete a few hours later when the elder Tarisio returned from work, boisterously happy because he had seen his son's horse and buggy as he rode up. He took his Luigi through the house, showing him all the work that had been accomplished during his absence. Then he sat down to talk to his son.

"So you go to Florence?" he asked.

Tarisio nodded. "There is a very fine violin there I wish to acquire," he said. "A very fine one."

Florence was not a safe place, the father said anxiously. There was trouble there, people were weary of the Grand Duke. Florence was a city of intrigue and murders.

"I know, Papa," Tarisio replied.

The father studied his son's face. Then he reached into

his pocket and brought out two odd-looking pieces of metal, a series of rings welded together with sharp points on the tops. He slipped a hand into one, his fingers fitting neatly into the connected rings. Then he doubled his fist and displayed it to his son. Tarisio whistled. This was a formidable weapon. With a single blow of the fist, a man could crush his adversary's face.

"For you," the father said. "At night be sure to wear them. They may save your life."

Tarisio pocketed the weapon and then showed his father a short stiletto that could fit neatly in his boot. With the knife and the iron rings, he said, he would be amply protected. He intended to leave for Florence the next day but first he wanted to see the violins his father had found at Chiaravalle. The old man was pleased, walked out of the room and returned in a moment, proudly laying two cases before his son.

A month earlier Luigi would have rushed to inspect the contents of the cases, but now the novelty of seeing Cremonas had worn off and he felt he could be magnanimous and permit his father the pleasure of displaying his treasures at leisure.

"You take them out, Father," he said.

The older man grinned, slipped the clasp off the case, and lifted out a thing of beauty in light golden varnish. Tarisio whistled and his father turned the violin around slowly, as he had seen his son do more than once, commenting, "Note the handsome curls of the back, the matching sides and head, the choice grain of the spruce top. Do you know the maker?"

"Guadagnini." Tarisio smiled. "Joannes Baptista Guadagnini."

"You know the date it says inside?" There was a frown

on the father's face and suspicion in his voice. The son knew a great deal more than he had thought.

Tarisio grinned. "No, Papa," he said. "The date I do not know; the maker yes. He has a style all his own."

Papa Tarisio peered through the F-holes and read the label. "Turin: 1776," he announced triumphantly. He reached for the second case, glancing shrewdly at his son. "I suppose," he remarked, "that you can tell the maker of this one by the case."

Tarisio laughed. "No, Papa," he replied. "You will have to show it to me."

The old man took the second violin out and held it up. "Now tell me," he challenged.

"Giovanni Grancino," Tarisio replied.

Papa Tarisio laughed and set the fiddle down. "I knew it, I knew it," he chortled. "I knew it. My boy, you can fool some people, but you cannot fool your father. This violin is not a Grancino!"

Tarisio was puzzled. "No?" he asked.

"No," the father insisted. "This is by Giovanni Baptista Rogeri, and a fine piece of work. Made in 1690. I can prove it." He handed the instrument to his son. "Read the label, and see for yourself."

Tarisio took the instrument and examined it painstakingly. Finally he peered into an F-hole and read the label. "Odd," he murmured, "extremely odd."

"Something wrong, Luigi?"

Tarisio nodded. "Yes, Father. The label says Rogeri, but this is not Rogeri's work. It is a Grancino."

"You are sure? How do you know?"

Tarisio explained patiently. "It is like this, Papa. You tell by the carving, by the workmanship, by the varnish.

Rogeri never made a violin like this, he was too much of a perfectionist."

The old man shrugged. "I suppose you must be right. So someone tried to perpetrate a fraud, but we lose nothing, my boy. We pay nothing for either of these fiddles. My friend, the monk at Chiaravalle, gave me these because I made a dresser for him to keep his things in. But it is only proper that a fraud should come from Chiaravalle, for after all, this is where the woman Guglielmina hatched her plan to be the Pope over all women, and tried to teach the heresy that she was the Holy Spirit incarnate in the feminine sex. Do you know, my son, that they never did a thing to her for that? She lived to be an old woman and they even buried her at Chiaravalle. Why, if you or I would have tried that, they'd have had us drawn and quartered!"

Tarisio patted his father affectionately on the shoulder. "It's all right, Papa, it's all right."

The old man arose. "We'll throw these violins away, no?"

Tarisio shook his head violently. "Papa," he said, "these are not fine Cremonas, but they are genuine, false labels or not. Believe me, they will fetch a pretty penny; not as much as a Strad, but a good price anyway."

The old man arose. "Well, my boy, I go to visit with Mama now."

*Florence in 1830*

# CHAPTER 16

ON THE SURFACE, Florence seemed serene when Tarisio arrived there one beautiful afternoon in June. The size and activity of the city impressed him, and although he already had become accustomed to the traffic of Paris and Milan, there was a distinctly different atmosphere in this city. He felt the undercurrents of unrest and desperate determination, and in the faces of the Florentines he fancied he could see trouble beneath the façade of opulence and elegance.

People laughed and joked, but everywhere, in the potpourri of street noises, he thought he detected a false note. There were troops here, the spectacularly uniformed officers of Leopold II, resplendent in braid and brass, and the ordinary men of the ranks, all intermingled with the crowds.

Tarisio had checked into a hotel in the Via Maggio, on the right bank of the River Arno which cut through the center of the city. The Ponte Santa Trinità, a sagging, ancient bridge that seemed on the verge of toppling into the river, stretched ahead of him.

Across the river there was the boom of cannon and the roar of rockets. It was a feast day, and Florence was celebrating the Festival of St. John.

By nightfall one might have thought the Guelphs had come back and started another war. Tarisio decided to cross the bridge and see the sights himself. He had no idea where the Count di Salabue lived, and he wanted to inquire of someone, but not at his hotel. It might be wiser if no one knew his mission in the city. He crossed the bridge in a stream of traffic, and as he neared the east shore the crowds became thicker. At the far end of the bridge he came upon an elderly man, pad and pencil in hand, sketching the enchanting river scene. The tempo of the fireworks was increasing and dusk was descending. The artist began to pack up his things.

"A thousand pardons," Tarisio began. The elderly man smiled pleasantly. "I am a stranger," Tarisio went on. "All those fireworks—where do they come from?"

"About twenty minutes' walk," the artist replied. "That is the start of the Festival of St. John in the Piazza Santa Maria Novella. If you want to see it close up, go straight ahead. The street leading off the east end of the bridge is the Via Tornabuoni. Walk down to its end, and you will be right in the middle of it."

Tarisio thanked the man and headed east. As he entered the Via Tornabuoni he was caught up in the crowd, headed in the same direction. The character of the street, with its paving of large slabs, changed as he walked along. Bookstores, banks, chemists' shops, small markets, all these mingled with an occasional theater and café. The mixture intrigued him, because he had never seen anything quite like it. In Milan, for instance, everything was grouped in orderly fashion—sections of the city for mercantile establishments, groups of restaurants vying with each other for attention, and market places one next to the other. But here it was different. A tobacconist's shop stood next door to a fish market, next to that a staid bank, and then a store which displayed clothing for women.

Then a window sign caught his attention: Ballerini & Figlio, Cloth Merchants. This was the firm the Count was said to operate clandestinely. Tarisio stared through the windows, marked the address in his mind, and strolled on.

It was dark by the time he returned to his hotel. The fireworks and gaiety of the festival crowds had thrilled and amused him, but now he had forgotten them. Tomorrow was to be a memorable day in his life, for he expected to find Le Messie, if the fabulous violin was still in existence. He lay down to sleep, but the climax of his quest was too near. He tossed for hours, and sleep did not come until nearly dawn.

He slept late, ate a leisurely breakfast, and started down the Via Maggio toward the other side of the city. As he walked toward the Ponte Santa Trinità he decided that he would be cautious in revealing his knowledge of the Count's connection with the cloth merchant's firm. He knew no one in Florence to whom he could turn in case of trouble. The city was filled with intrigue, and the Count was an important person with powerful connections. If he so desired, he could easily have Luigi thrown into a dungeon. It was well known that the Florentine nobility ruled with an iron fist.

But how to play his cards? How to use his knowledge of Di Salabue's business connections without creating a hazard to his own safety? It was a ticklish question. Should he leave a sealed letter at the hotel as a guarantee of his freedom and safety? He dismissed the idea as worthless.

What good could such a letter do? Even if its contents were revealed, the Count could easily shrug them off as the raving of a madman. His knowledge appeared more of a liability than an asset.

Tarisio had reached the bridge when he remembered that he had left behind the Amati with which he hoped to bait Di Salabue. He retraced his steps to the hotel, picked up the violin, and headed again for the other side of Florence. When he neared the east end of the Ponte Santa Trinità he stopped at a small cart laden with articles of leather and picked up a pair of women's gloves, ostensibly examining the workmanship, but eyeing the peddler carefully. He bought the gloves and casually asked for directions to the Count's home. The man looked at him boldly, and Tarisio became uncomfortable. It seemed to him that all Florentines had a disconcerting directness about them.

The way to the house of Di Salabue was simple. Tarisio was to go straight up the Via Tornabuoni to the Via Strozzi. At the intersection of the two streets was the Palazzo Strozzi, a stone building as strong as a fortress, three stories high and the largest structure there. The house of Di Salabue was next door, a much smaller place, but dignified and impressive.

Tarisio walked on, fiddle case under his arm, his thoughts in a turmoil. He wished now that he had never heard that the Count had business connections, and that business was a forbidden word with nobility. All he wanted was to buy a violin, without the complications which now seemed to be strangling him. In this frame of mind he reached the firm of Ballerini & Figlio, which he had passed the night before, and on the spur of the moment walked in.

"I am a stranger in Florence," he told a handsome, pleasant-looking youth. "Can you direct me to the home of Count Cozio di Salabue?"

The young man was instantly cordial. "I am his grandson," he replied. "And you?"

Tarisio had come to Florence expecting deception and intrigue and the young man's candor took him by surprise. The youth saw the incredulity in Tarisio's face as he introduced himself. "Permit me to explain," he continued quickly. "The Count owns this firm. There is a new era in Florence. The nobility has gone to work." He chuckled. "Are you a friend of the Count?"

Tarisio shook his head. "I have never met him," he replied. "But I have heard of his great interest in violins, and I have a very fine Amati to show him."

The youth reached for his hat and coat. "Come," he said laughingly. "If you have an Amati, my grandfather will be overjoyed to see you. Nowadays that is his great passion, and I will be in his good graces for bringing you to him."

Bewildered, Tarisio followed the young man. The transition from his preconceived notions of difficulty and intrigue to the realities of the situation overwhelmed him.

On the walk up the Via Tornabuoni, the young man chatted pleasantly. His grandfather was a great lover of violins, he said, but he was getting old. He was nearly eighty, and, the grandson suspected, might be happy to see his collection in the right hands. But almost every day he changed his mind about selling it. Some days he grumbled because the violins were a nuisance, and other days he hovered over them as though they were his most precious possessions.

Tarisio guardedly asked: "Does he have any favorites?"

The young man grinned. "Not really," he said. "But there *was* one in particular."

Tarisio's heart seemed to leap into his throat. Had something happened to Le Messie?

There was one, the young man rambled on, that the Count desired above all others. This was an Amati that had been made by Stradivari when he was an apprentice. But he never got this instrument. Through some error it was never delivered to him although he had ordered it.

Tarisio had difficulty in suppressing his upsurge of joy. He could have shouted with relief. Under his arm was the very instrument Di Salabue's grandson was talking about!

The two passed the Palazzo Strozzi and stopped at the next house. The young man rapped smartly on the door. A small square panel in the door opened, a face peered out, and then the door instantly swung open. To Tarisio it was like stepping into a strange new world. Word was sent to the Count that he had a visitor, and as he waited in the reception room, Tarisio looked around. Beneath his feet was deep, green carpeting interlaced with figuring. Oil paintings framed in highly burnished bronze hung on the walls, and over the mantel of a marble fireplace hung the almost life-sized portrait of an elderly man. Tarisio guessed it was one of the Count's ancestors and that it had been painted two or three hundred years earlier. Muted light filtered through stained-glass windows, bordered with green drapes that matched the carpeting.

The door opened, and an old, but still erect, man entered. "I am Count Cozio di Salabue," he said, extending his hand. "And you are Luigi Tarisio." It was a matter-of-fact statement, but the way he said it made it sound as though Tarisio was the most important man in Italy.

*Count Cozio di Salubue*

# AUX AMATEURS

## DE MUSIQUE

Un amateur de musique aïant fait depuis plusieurs années avec beaucoup de soin et de dépense une ample et choisie collection de Violons des plus célebrés Auteurs Crémonois qui aient jamais été, tels que Antoine, Jerome, et Nicolas Amatis Pere, oncle et Fils, Antoine Stradivario, Rugeri dit le Per, Andrée et Joseph Guarnerio, Charles Bergonzio, et Jean Baptiste Guadagnini, et étant disposé à vendre cette collection tant en gros, qu'en détail ici à Milan, avant de satisfaire aux demandes qu'on lui a faites hors du païs, cet amateur invite tous ceux qui en voudront faire acquisition de s'adresser dans l'espace de 20. jours à dater du 22. prairial tous les jours ouvriers depuis les onze heures du matin jusqu'à midi, et depuis les trois heures après-midi jusqu'à cinq, au portier de la maison 1295. dans la Rue *del Gesù* peu loin du mont S. Thérese, qui leur fera voir cette collection aux heures et jours ci devant marqués.

Cet amateur se flatte que non seulement ils admireront la rareté de cette collection, mais qu'ils trouveront encore très-discrets les prix qui y sont fixés, en égard aux qualités de ces instrumens.

Milan ce 22. Prairial An. IX. Republicain. ( 8. Juin 1801. v. s. ).

# To the Virtuosos of Violins.

*A Virtuoso having done a large, and choice collection of Violins of most famous ancient Cremone's Authors, viz, of* Anthony, Jerom, *and* Nicolas Amatis, Antohny Stradivarius, Francis Ruger, *called* Per, Andreas *and* Joseph Guarnerius, Charles Bergonzi, *and* John Baptist Guadagnini, *and being now disposed to sell that collection both by wholesale, and separately here into Milan, at discret price, invites all virtuosos who will buy them, to apply in this City to Merchant Anthony Clerici at house Cavanago in the street of that name, N. 2334 since twelve o' clock until two, and since four, until six.*

*The Count's announcement for the sale of his instruments*

Luigi nodded, gulped in embarrassment, and mumbled, "I am honored, Your Highness."

Di Salabue smiled. "Not 'Your Highness,'" he corrected gently. "I am referred to as 'Your Excellency.' Come join me in my study." Tarisio glanced from the painting on the wall to the Count and back again. The likeness was remarkable. Di Salabue smiled. "That is a painting of my great-grandfather. I see also that you are surprised that I should know your name. I have been expecting you to call for a long time, for I have heard of your collecting of Cremonas."

He led the way into a nearby room and Tarisio stopped spellbound on the threshold. Resting securely on brackets against the farthest wall were eleven of the most beautiful Stradivaris he had ever seen.

The Count watched him closely. "Lovely, aren't they?"

Tarisio nodded, his eyes searching for Le Messie. Over and over they probed the fiddles on the wall, but none fitted the description of the one he sought. Bergonzi's warning words echoed in his mind: *The man is a fox, you will have to be on your toes.*

He turned around, the picture of urbanity. "A beautiful collection, Your Excellency. Certainly the finest Stradivari violins I have seen. They must give you great pleasure."

The Count smiled, and behind his gold-rimmed glasses Tarisio thought he detected the glint of slyness. This was a game of cat and mouse, Tarisio thought. The man was not going to mention Le Messie until he had to.

"Yes," the nobleman said affably, "I am quite proud of these instruments. I went to considerable trouble to get them from the Stradivari family. But now, let me see the Amati my grandson tells me you brought."

This was it, Tarisio thought. This was his chance to

charm the old gentleman. He looked around the room, mindful of Vuillaume's advice concerning the art of exhibiting a Cremona: *Set the stage,* Vuillaume had said. *Take it to a window where the sun can be your ally, or beneath a bright light.* He gestured to a window. "I should like that drapery closed tightly," he said, "and this one," indicating the nearest window, "drawn open. Then I should like the door to your study shut so that we may have uninterrupted privacy."

A servant quickly carried out Tarisio's request. With all the dignity at his command, and much like an artist about to take the center of the stage, Luigi opened the case. He lifted the Amati gently and walked to the window. Holding it between his two palms, one pressing the tip of the scroll and the other the bottom rib of the violin, he slowly revolved it in the beam of sunshine. Then, with no comment whatsoever, he handed it to the Count.

He could hear Di Salabue suck in his breath as he grasped it, fingering the delicate neck and head, sliding his fingertips over the richly varnished back; and he knew he had won, that all he had to do now was to be patient.

The Count finally put the Amati down, and there was a note of reverence in his voice as he said: "This is the last violin Stradivari ever worked on during his apprenticeship to the Amatis, but there is no doubt in my mind that it is the finest Amati ever made. Why they let a mere youth work on it is something we will never know. What do you suppose Stradivari actually had to do with this particular violin?"

Tarisio shrugged. "Who can say?" he replied. "Perhaps all he ever did was to rub down the varnish. The workmanship certainly is too characteristic of Amati to be anyone else's."

Di Salabue idly plucked a string and it gave off a clear, soft note. Pure and silvery, the tone brought an expression of ecstasy to the Count's face. He sat down and gestured Tarisio to a chair. "We Florentines can be quite blunt and to the point," he began. "Permit me to begin by saying that I want this Amati."

Tarisio nodded. "Understandable," he murmured.

"The Stradivaris are very fine," the Count went on, "but, as you know, I have a penchant for the Amati. Now, some of us like the creations of Duccio, and others the work of Raphael. This is a matter of personal feeling, as both are great. The preference of one means no rejection of the other. This is my feeling as regards the Amati and the Stradivari."

"With a person of your stature," Tarisio replied diplomatically, "this preference can be a very potent matter. For instance, were your preference for the Amati generally known, then all Cremonese violins except the Amati could become next to worthless. Therefore, in the interests of those unfortunate enough to possess Stradivaris, perhaps you should not be too single-minded in your devotion to the Amatis."

Tarisio had scored a bull's-eye.

Di Salabue tugged at the corner of his white mustache and there was a twinkle in his eye as he realized the trap into which he had stepped. He reached for a decanter of wine. "I propose," he said, "to drink to a very astute young trader in violins."

Tarisio lifted his glass and murmured: "And I to a most generous patron of the arts."

The Count sipped his wine and leaned forward in his chair. "And now, the Amati," he said firmly.

Tarisio avoided a direct answer. "I had heard," he

ventured, "that you acquired twelve violins from Paolo Stradivari. I see only eleven. Has one been lost?"

The Count peered closely at Tarisio, saw nothing revealing in his expressionless face, and smiled. "There is another," he admitted. "A rather unusual one, but unusual only in that it has never been played. Would you like to see it?"

Without waiting for a reply he went to a chest Tarisio had noticed earlier, raised the lid, and took out a violin which he put on a low table in front of his visitor. Tarisio stared at it. This was Le Messie—Stradivari's masterpiece. He felt a cold chill in his arms and legs. He tried to speak, but his voice cracked and quavered like that of an aged man.

There was triumph in the Count's face, and when he spoke his voice was hard and brittle with the snap of someone who knows that he holds the trump card. "I make you this proposal," he said crisply. "Your Amati and four thousand French francs for all of my Stradivaris."

Tarisio could only nod his head, and after a moment or so, like a man going through an action without fully realizing what he was doing, he counted out four thousand francs and put them down on the table beside his Amati. The Count quickly scooped up the money, stuffed it into his waistcoat, and, picking up the Amati, vanished from the room.

In a few moments a servant arrived to tell Tarisio that the Count begged his indulgence, since he was somewhat indisposed; would Tarisio avail himself of the assistance of the household staff to remove his violins? Tarisio picked up Le Messie and slowly put it into its case. By the time he had finished, the servant was waiting with the other violins.

Within fifteen minutes Tarisio was back in his hotel room, and the only thing that made him realize that he had not dreamed it all was the twelve violin boxes stacked up in a corner. Suddenly he became aware of a small white envelope tied to the lock of one of the cases. Inside, on a small sheet bearing the crest of the house of Di Salabue, he read:

My dear Tarisio:
    Obviously you have been enchanted by the magic of Cremona. Should you ever come to Florence again, by all means call on me.
                                              Di Salabue
P.S. Mark you, that twelfth Stradivari shall affect you strangely.

Tarisio dropped the note. It was clear to him now that the Count had not realized that this twelfth violin in his collection was Le Messie. To him it was merely a strange, fascinating instrument, no more than one of the few Stradivaris known to have come directly from its maker's hands. But he had capitalized on Tarisio's desire. Luigi opened the box to gloat over his treasure. Le Messie was everything Sister Francesca had said it was and more, and even Bergonzi's description had not done it justice.

To Tarisio it seemed incredible that this creation should now be his. He stared long at the violin and as he looked, the color seemed to leap forward from the very grain. He had the sensation that his fingers were wet and sticky with varnish. Even the brush marks appeared to flow together in a silky, smooth coat. His eyes searched for the nick of a chisel, or a knife. No wood surface could be carved or finished so perfectly without rubbing. It seemed incredible, but there was no vestige of this. He turned the instrument over, exploring every detail of the grain in the wood. Le Messie seemed to be speaking to him, and there, all alone in a strange hotel room in a foreign city, the burden of his possession suddenly overcame him. He did not really possess Le Messie. The violin possessed him.

He was startled when he realized how long he had been staring at the instrument. When he looked out of the window, he found that evening had come.

During the night a strange metamorphosis seemed to overtake him. When he awakened, he found that the madness of the quest had vanished, in its place there was a troubled feeling where there should have been serenity— a desire for something new in life instead of the relentless quest of Cremonas. He felt that he would like to stay in Florence, bask in its beauty and its colorful way of life; yet he knew that he must go on and on, pursuing the manifestations of Cremona's art until each last bit had been found and restored to its proper place.

A little while later he was on his way again, headed back to Milan.

*William Moennig II holding "Le Messie"*

*Piazza del Duomo, Milan*

# CHAPTER 17

THE CONSTRAST BETWEEN Milan and Florence assailed Tarisio's eyes and ears when he turned into the Corso Roma. The traffic was heavier, and the people different, and Tarisio saw the Milanese in sharp contrast to the suave, well-dressed Florentines.

He passed the Duomo, turned into the Via Broletto, rode up the Via Mercato and Via Tivoli, and then past the park into the Via Legnano. Workmen were transforming one end of the park into a brick-walled arena. Tarisio stopped to watch them for a minute, and then drove to his place at the end of the street. The boxes of violins were bulky and heavy, but rather than ask for assistance he decided to manage them himself. Upstairs in his attic he unpacked his treasures, and toyed with the idea of making a written inventory of all his violins, but decided against it. He knew every fiddle he owned, as well as the circumstances under which he had acquired them, and to him that was sufficient. Perhaps later, when he had stuffed his room with Cremonas, he might take time to list them.

He had unpacked Le Messie first, but would not hang

that instrument like the others. Le Messie would have a special place. He opened the bottom drawer of the highboy, carefully padded it with rags, and then laid his treasure there. It was a good, safe place, because the highboy was a sturdy piece of chestnut furniture. Patting the violin affectionately, he gently shut the drawer and turned his attention to the other violins the Count had sold him. All were in prime condition, and would fetch a neat price. The thought of money turned his mind to his pocket book. He had been spending lavishly and it was time to take stock. He found that he had little more than three thousand francs left—just enough to get him back to Paris in style. Tarisio selected eighteen violins and gathered up the five dismantled Cremonas Bergonzi had given him. They would go to Paris without being reassembled, because he would not have time now to restore them. He was too busy.

It was good to have a friend like Vuillaume, Tarisio thought, but even so he could foresee when the value of Cremonas might become entirely a question of supply and demand, and he intended to make certain that the supply would always be meagre. If Vuillaume or anyone else wanted the seven Strads he was taking to Paris, he decided, they would have to buy the eleven lesser instruments, too: a Guarneri, a Rogeri, several Gaglianos, a Storioni, a Balestrieri, a violin with the label of Michael Plattner, the Grancino his father had found, and several others. The plan struck Tarisio as shrewd. The Strads would bring real money. The others? He shrugged. He'd make the most of them.

Tarisio locked up, carried his violins downstairs, and started for Fontanetto, deciding to stop on the way to buy lumber. He wanted to build a large box in which to pack the instruments for the trip to France. Papa Tarisio could help him, and then, after a few days' rest, he would start out for Paris, where French francs, thousands of them, waited for his arrival.

The idea of acquiring wealth intrigued Tarisio for the first time, and as he rode toward Fontanetto the thought struck him that perhaps this was one of the things he really wanted in life—money, and the power and luxury that went with it. It conjured up in his mind visions of himself dressed in the finest clothes, a man who could mingle with important people, even with royalty. He might even hire a tutor to teach him the fine points of being a gentleman.

The next few days were easy and lazy. Tarisio slept long and late, and gorged himself on his mother's cooking. Could he have peered into the future he might have changed his plans and lingered, because this was destined to be the last time he would ever spend with his parents. He talked by the hour of the money he intended to make, and, little by little, a new feeling about him began to come upon his mother. She saw her son in a different light. Luigi had changed. Was it good, this desire for money? Was it good that he was so determined to get it? Among the Italian peasants of the time, money and evil were synonymous. She wondered whether Tarisio would possess money or whether money would possess him. But whatever her thoughts, she kept them to herself; not even to her husband, happy in his new life on the farm, did she confide her fears.

Tarisio's father helped him build a large box and the violins were placed into it, firmly packed in straw. "I don't know how long I'll be away, Papa," Luigi said when the job was completed. "But don't worry, I will write and send money." Papa Tarisio just smiled and nodded, but there was a moistness in his eyes as he listened, for Luigi was the apple of his eye.

In the morning Tarisio was gone, and he never again saw his parents alive.

*Display of Italian violins of the 17th and 18th centuries*

*Paris scene*

*Paris scene*

# CHAPTER 18

TARISIO ARRRIVED IN PARIS two weeks later, after a leisurely trip over a new route and a stopover in Turin.
All along the way he had heard talk of the new railroad.
Everyone said that in another year or two the stagecoach
would be a thing of the past. Austria had been laying track
for two years, and in France thousands of workmen had
been grading the right of way and putting down miles of
twin ribbons of rail. The project fascinated Tarisio. Soon
he might make the trip from Milan to Paris in a few days,
and there were advantages to that; but the railroad would
be of no use to him in his search for fiddles. To reach
the hinterlands of Italy there was only one satisfactory
vehicle—the horse and buggy.

He found Paris unchanged. After unloading his box of
violins, he ordered a hackney and headed for Vuillaume's
place. He had momentary qualms about dropping in unexpectedly, and wished that he had written Vuillaume his
time of arrival. But the doubts vanished as soon as the
hackney turned into Vuillaume's drive. Vehicles lined
the driveway, and there was considerable movement on

the grounds. Tarisio grinned. It was Thursday afternoon, and he would walk right into the middle of his friend's hocus-pocus of varnishing violins in the greenhouse!

A servant helped unload his large box. Tarisio paid the driver, and then strolled across the spacious lawn to the greenhouse. The scene resembled a carnival. Fully fifty men and women crowded the greenhouse, and in the center, standing on a foot-high platform, his bald head gleaming brightly in the sun, stood Vuillaume, busily varnishing a violin. Tarisio edged his way into the group to hear better. The Frenchman was saying:

"I have found that the most satisfactory way to apply varnish is the simplest. I use this inch-and-a-half camel-hair brush and merely dip the tip into the varnish—so. Then I spread it in a very thin coat. This will minimize the chances of the varnish running and forming ridges. You will note that I varnish only a small portion of surface at a time." He twirled the violin around in his fingers, letting his audience see that one side remained white, and that he had only varnished a small part. "When I have applied the varnish," he continued, "I hang the violin up to dry."

A spectator spoke up. "How many coats do you recommend?"

"I use four," Vuillaume replied. "I have it on the best authority that the great Stradivari used this very method."

Suddenly he caught sight of Tarisio's grinning face in the audience. Putting down his brush, he announced abruptly: "That will be all for today." He picked up the three violins that he had varnished during his demonstration, stepped down, shouted a greeting to his friend, and called to him to follow as he started out for his house at a dogtrot.

Tarisio caught up to him with a few steps. "Why the rush?" he asked.

"I'm so happy to see you, Tarisio," Vuillaume bubbled. "But let's hurry. Some of this stuff is beginning to set, and I have to get it off before it starts to harden."

Twenty minutes later, the violins wiped clean, Vuillaume sat down to catch his breath. "They kept me talking so long down there today," he laughed, "that I thought I'd never be able to clean these violins up in time."

"But why?" Tarisio asked.

There was a trace of petulance in Vuillaume's face. "These are my own creations," he said, "and I think they are good. But this spirit varnish—well, it won't do for me; for the amateurs yes. Paris is full of amateur violinmakers these days, and the advertising I get this way is good for my business. When they fail—and they always do—they come to me to buy."

Tarisio nodded. "Good business," he grunted.

Vuillaume jumped from his chair and clapped Luigi on the shoulder. "And you, my friend—you look wonderful and successful!"

"I brought eighteen Cremonas with me," Tarisio replied, "and five more which have been dismantled. They are downstairs."

Hours later, after Vuillaume had calmed down and catalogued each instrument, he and Tarisio sat down to talk. Contrary to Tarisio's earlier feeling, Vuillaume was keenly interested in the lesser violins, particularly the Rogeri and the Gaglianas.

"Obviously, Luigi," he said, "the Rogeri and the Gaglianas are not in the same class with the Stradivaris, but nevertheless they are fine instruments."

Tarisio heaved a sigh of relief. "I am glad to hear you say that," he replied, "because I had made up my mind not to part with the Strads unless I could sell the others too."

Then the two men discussed the instruments Bergonzi had dismantled. Vuillaume was full of questions about the old man. "Is he still making violins?" he asked.

Tarisio nodded. "A few," he said. "But he is discouraged and bitter. He feels that he is a failure."

Vuillaume sighed. "That is the penalty of following in the path of an illustrious ancestor. One never quite measures up. The original Carlo was one of the greatest—in Stradivari's class. By the way, has Chanot written you about finding the top of a Stradivari cello in Spain?"

"Yes," Tarisio replied. "Only he didn't go into too many details."

Vuillaume gave his friend the story, and Luigi listened with interest. But then his thoughts returned to the dismantled Cremonas he had brought with him, and he mentioned them to Vuillaume. Vuillaume shook his head. He couldn't handle them, because there were too many other things to do. But he had a suggestion. Why not offer them to Chanot, who would jump at the chance to get them?

Tarisio thought it an excellent idea and at once the two men, with the dismantled Stradivaris securely packed, rode over to see Chanot, who was delighted to meet the Italian again.

The conversation quickly turned to the cello top. Chanot brought it out, and Tarisio, his eyes gleaming, examined the results of Ortego's butchery. The top was in better shape than he had anticipated, and although the varnish had been blistered by its contact with the sun, the damage was not extensive. Fine pumice stone and a polishing rag could remedy it.

Tarisio pinched a small blister with his fingernail and brought up a flake of varnish about the size of his thumb, which he displayed to Vuillaume. "Feel it," he urged, "and tell me what sensation you get."

Vuillaume rubbed the flake of varnish lightly between thumb and forefinger, the frown on his forehead deepening. He gave Tarisio an odd look. "Spirit varnish?" he asked incredulously. "Can it be that Stradivari used two types on his work—gum varnish and a spirit varnish?"

"I've long suspected it," Tarisio replied.

Chanot took the flake and touched it with the tip of his tongue. "It has a rosin-like taste," he commented. "But how can you be certain that Stradivari applied this? Perhaps Ortego put it on!"

"You are absolutely right," Tarisio agreed. "No one really knows. But it certainly raises an interesting point and one which we should all watch for. Everyone would like to know the secret of the master's varnish. This may be a clew. And now, about this top. Is it mine?"

Chanot flushed, then said: "When I wrote to you, Tarisio, I intended to present it to you. But I must be frank—I really cannot afford to give it away."

"I'll pay one thousand francs," Tarisio replied. "Enough?"

"More than fair," Chanot murmured. "Vuillaume, what do you say?"

"I agree," the Frenchman replied. It was a generous price, he thought. After all, Tarisio must first locate the rest of the instrument, manage to acquire it, and then hope that it could be restored to its original condition.

Tarisio excused himself and went to get his package. Then, while Chanot watched curiously, he cleared off a place on a nearby table and piled the violin parts in five stacks.

Chanot drew in his breath sharply. "They're real," he shouted. "And perfectly disassembled! Who did this magnificent job? A little glue—that's all that is needed; there is not a nick, not a crack!"

Tarisio and Vuillaume smiled at each other.

"Permit me to explain, Chanot," Tarisio began. "Some years ago my friend, the grandson of Carlo Bergonzi, tried to unmask the mystery of Stradivari. He took these violins apart, making exact reproductions, but he never had time nor the inclination to reassemble them, and so here they are, in their original state. In return for your selling me your cello top, I offer you these five instruments for one thousand francs each. Restore them, and they will fetch you many, many times that amount."

Chanot looked thunderstruck.

"Spare your voice, my friend," Tarisio continued smoothly, "and simply permit the francs to flutter down into my hand. That will be expression enough."

Chanot and Vuillaume looked as though they thought Tarisio was joking. It took a long time to convince them otherwise, but at last the transaction was concluded.

Tarisio spent the next several days sightseeing and visiting with Vuillaume. The latter had quickly notified various people that he could now fill their requests for Cremonas. Seventeen of the Cremonas brought a total of seventy-three thousand francs. For the time being Tarisio kept one Guarneri.

Vuillaume offered his friend some advice. "I would suggest," he said, "that you deposit most of this money in one of the banks. Carry ten thousand, that will be ample for your immediate needs. A letter of credit for the balance will serve as well as cash."

"An excellent idea," Tarisio commented. "Before I go to Spain, however, there are other matters I should like to discuss with you."

"I am all ears," Vuillaume replied.

"Well," Tarisio began, "I have many more violins, but I hesitate to bring so many to France at one time. Perhaps it would be wiser if I came, from now on, with only a few."

A foxy glint which Tarisio had once before seen in Vuillaume's eyes now reappeared. "Shrewd," Vuillaume murmured. "Shrewd. The appetite is whetted, but the food is withheld. Very shrewd. Now I have some news for you, my great detective. There was one violin made by Stradivari that was so perfect that it was called Le Messie. Recently I received word that King George of England would possess this perfect work of art. Do you know what that means?"

Tarisio's face was inscrutable. "What does it mean," he asked softly, "other than that he desires to possess it?"

Vuillaume leaned forward and tapped Tarisio on the knee. "It means," he replied, "that you could get a king's ransom for it. Perhaps half a million francs. But, of course, you do not have it. And who knows where it is? Between 1716 and today many things could have happened to it. Chances are it no longer exists."

Tarisio apparently had not been listening. He stared dreamily out the window, deep in reverie. When he finally turned back to Vuillaume he said:

"Vuillaume, on your word of honor, will you keep faith with me if I share a secret with you?"

The Frenchman nodded.

"I have Le Messie," Tarisio said simply. "One day I may

bring it to Paris. But not yet. It is truly the ultimate of the violinmaker's art. To see it is to experience a thrill such as one has never known. It has never been played, has known neither rosin nor a bow, yet it will sing, someday, with the voice of the Lord."

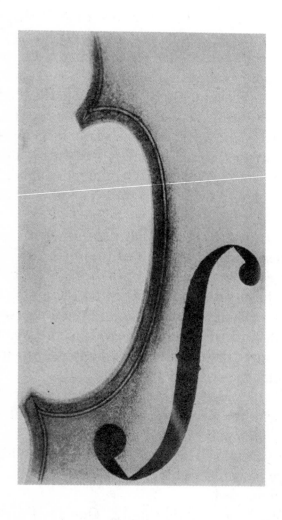

*Detail of "Le Messie"*

*Stradivari as depicted in "The Master" by John Rae*

*Ole Bull in his early years*

# CHAPTER 19

THE STORY OF THE Bass of Spain had delighted Tarisio. He was impatient to start for Madrid, intending, in fact, to leave the very next day, but unexpected events interrupted his plans. Vuillaume, meanwhile, had discreetly refrained from questioning Tarisio further about Le Messie, deciding to bide his time until circumstances were more favorable.

That night an unexpected caller appeared at Vuillaume's home. It was Ole Bull, the young Norwegian violinist whose playing had created a sensation in Milan, Trieste, Bologna, and Paris, and who had known Vuillaume for some time. Tarisio had heard the Norwegian play and in his own mind compared the blond giant to Paganini. He recalled how enchanted he had been with Ole Bull's skill. In Bologna the Norwegian had won the hearts of his audience when, as an encore, he played *Norma*, the *Siege of Corinth*, and *Romeo and Juliet*, uniting melodies from the three operas into a single improvisation. Tarisio had heard him.

Italians loved that sort of thing, and Tarisio was no

exception. Another thing that had caught his fancy was Ole Bull's favorite trick of using a flat bridge on his violin, so that he could play all four strings at one time.

From stories he had heard, Tarisio expected to meet a freak, and he was pleasantly surprised. The Norwegian— tall, handsome, and poised—was a far cry from the ruffian Tarisio had imagined him to be, even though, at that moment, he was very agitated.

"It's my fiddle," Ole Bull cried to Vuillaume. "My Seraphin is played out! I must have another at once!" Vuillaume nodded understandingly. He knew what Ole Bull meant; fine instruments, like the artists who performed on them, became "tired" from constant use, and required rest to regain their responsiveness.

Ole Bull wanted a Guarneri such as his idol Paganini was using. He had heard about Vuillaume finding a Guarneri for Paganini and he wanted to know if the Frenchman could do the same for him.

"Quite recently, after I had been up all night, I composed an *Adagio Religioso*. It is quite an effective piece, involving all sorts of technical difficulties, and tomorrow I play it. I must have a Guarneri."

Vuillaume, who had not yet had an opportunity to introduce Tarisio, opened his mouth, but the artist spoke again before he could utter a word.

"I know Guarneris are almost impossible to find. But I simply must have one. I need an instrument with a big voice. I read in the newspapers some time ago that an Italian had brought a number to Paris. Perhaps you could find this fellow and persuade him to get me one."

Vuillaume managed to break in at last. "Ole," he said laughingly, gesturing to the man in the corner, "your worries are over. Meet Luigi Tarisio, the Italian you are so anxious to see. He has so many Cremonas he doesn't know what to do with them."

Tarisio and the Norwegian shook hands, and each took an instantaneous liking to the other. The three chatted for several hours and Ole Bull told how, when he had first come to Paris, he had soon run out of money, but through luck had won a considerable amount at the Frascati club. This had a special interest for Tarisio, because, he recalled, Aldric had tried to send him there when he first came to Paris. Perhaps, Tarisio commented, if he had accepted Aldric's suggestion he might have won his fortune much faster than he ever could hunting old violins.

Then Vuillaume told about the Guarneri copy he was making for Paganini, and boasted that when it was finished Paganini himself would not be able to tell the difference between the original and the copy.

Tarisio laughed heartily. "I wager the best dinner in Paris," he said, "that you will find it an impossible task."

"Agreed," snapped Vuillaume. "And Ole Bull is our witness."

To Tarisio's regret, the friendly chat drew to a close and the moment for business arrived. He went to his room and returned with the Guarneri which he had refused to sell earlier. Ole Bull fell in love with it at sight and when he put a bow to it, his joy knew no bounds. The violin sang with a strong, clear, melodious voice that enchanted the player and his listeners. Tarisio urged him to try it out for a few days but the artist would not hear of it. He knew what he wanted, and this was it. He bought it on the spot.

"Before I leave," he said, "I would like to know how you recognize a true Guarneri. Or is this a presumptuous question?"

Vuillaume said nothing, but anyone could see that the same question had been on his mind, too. Tarisio was gracious about it. This was a secret of his calling, he said, but he had no objection to revealing it; as a matter of fact, he was flattered by Ole Bull's interest in his work.

Of all the Cremona masters, Tarisio explained, the work of Joseph del Gesu Guarneri was the easiest to recognize, because nature herself had placed her perpetual trademark on it. When the Guarneri family first set up shop in Cremona, they had acquired a fine piece of pine wood noted for its tonal qualities. The Guarneris made all their bellies or tops from this piece. Down the center of this plank there was a long strip which nature had overimpregnated with turpentine resin. As a result, this wood had a large dark stripe impossible to duplicate by artificial means.

"In other words," Vuillaume put in, "this is something no one could copy."

Tarisio nodded and continued his explanation. Each top the Guarneris made had this dark stripe in the center, and it was so brilliant that it could be detected through the beautiful yellow varnish for which the Guarneris were noted. He took the instrument from Ole Bull, and as the violinist stood beside him, held the Guarneri at arm's length, with the light at their backs. There was the trademark nature had bestowed upon the Guarneri family—a perfectly straight, off-color band of color about a quarter of an inch wide, that extended the entire length of the top.

Then Tarisio pointed to other features that distinguished the violin, and his knowledge fascinated Ole Bull. Almost all of the wood Guarneri used, Tarisio went on, had been cut *sur maille*—on the quarter. The deal of the belly was well chosen, the varnish always of excellent complexion and elastic quality. The slightly elevated arching subsided to a gentle curve to the purfling, and all the inner parts were made of excellent pine. These, Tarisio said, were the characteristics a connoisseur could find in a Guarneri.

However, there came a time in Guarneri's life when he no longer could make an acceptable violin. And near the end of his career, his work appeared to be no more than the degenerate fruit of a great talent rotted away.

Guarneri, Tarisio said, lived an irregular and dissolute life. Bergonzi had told the collector many of the details. According to Bergonzi, Guarneri was idle and negligent, loved wine and pleasure, and had even been confined to prison, where he had died in 1745 at the age of sixty-two.

There were stories, too, that while in prison the gaoler's daughter had furnished him with wood and wretched tools. She also acted as his agent, buying varnish from other makers. Tarisio did not believe these stories of Guarneri's career in prison, he said, but pointed out that they had been circulated widely.

"Nonetheless," he told his audience, "many other makers tried to imitate him—men like Paul Anthony Testore of Milan, Laurence Storioni of Cremona, and Charles Ferdinand Landolfi."

Vuillaume said: "I heard once that Guarneri was an illegitimate child and that this spurred on his genius."

"This is not so," Tarisio answered. "He was the legitimate son of John Baptiste Guarneri and Angela Maria Locadella. He was born in Cremona on June 8, 1683, and baptized in the parish of St. Donato at the Chapel of Ease of the cathedral. I myself have seen the records, and I could go on all night about the Guarneri family."

Even Vuillaume, expert as he was on the subject, was,

impressed. More and more he appreciated the true worth of Tarisio, not only as a collector, but as the sole living link between the dead era of Cremona's greatness, and the present. Someday, he reflected, the history of this art would owe much to the modest Italian. It was a prophetic thought.

In the morning there were new callers at Vuillaume's home, and for the time being, Tarisio put off his trip to Spain. John Hart, famous in England as a maker of violins and as a dealer, had just heard of Tarisio and had come rushing to Paris to see him. England hungered for Amatis, Stradivaris, Bergonzis, Guarneris, and other instruments of the Cremona school, and Hart was eager to establish contact with the young Italian.

The meeting at Vuillaume's place was amusing. Hart could speak no French, Vuillaume knew no English, and Hart, unaware that Tarisio knew English and French almost as well as he knew Italian, had brought along John Lott, an itinerant British violinmaker, to act as an interpreter; but Lott's cockney accent was so pronounced that Tarisio could not understand him, so Lott tried his French on Vuillaume. It, too, failed miserably, and the four men sat in Vuillaume's parlor utterly confounded.

Finally on impulse, Tarisio addressed a question to Lott in Italian, and the little Englishman, who barely topped five feet, broke into a broad smile. He had learned Italian, he said, while a member of a traveling theatrical troupe which featured a female elephant. Then, to the dismay of Hart and Vuillaume, he began an animated story of his career, which Tarisio, already charmed by the effervescence of this little man, found fascinating.

When he was sixteen or seventeen, Lott said, his mother died and his father married a woman whom he disliked,

so he left home and apprenticed himself to an English
violinmaker for no reason other than that there was nothing better to do. After a few months at his new trade he
made several violins and sold them. However, he soon
learned that the art of violinmaking involved tedious work
and did not pay well, so he tried other fields of endeavor.
One day, destitute and at the end of his rope, he applied
for a job as a member of a theater orchestra.

"I couldn't play a single note," he confided to Tarisio,
"but I had to eat."

"How could you do that?" Tarisio asked.

Lott grinned. It had been a simple deception. As a violinmaker he had learned to tune the instrument, but that
was the extent of his skill. However, he knew a trick or
two, so he talked the conductor into hiring him. He was
given a chair and sat down, promptly tuning his violin
louder than anyone else in the orchestra, conscious that
the conductor's eye was upon him. When the rest of the
orchestra stopped tuning up, Lott put his bow down and
quickly grabbed up a substitute bow. Then, with the conductor's full attention on him, Lott bowed through an
entire selection with graceful sweeps of his arm.

Convinced that he had found a new virtuoso, and delighted with his discovery, the conductor threw his arms
around Lott and wanted to move him into the first chair,
but Lott, too wise to risk being shown up, disdained the
promotion.

"But how did you get away with it, not knowing a single note?" Tarisio exclaimed.

Lott laughed uproariously. "You should have seen the
vibrato in my left hand," he shouted. "It was simply mar-
vellous—even Paganini would have envied me! But there
was nothing to fear. I had so much grease on that second

bow that it never made a sound. I kept my job in that orchestra for almost a year. The Adelphi Theater never had a finer artist!"

Tarisio was laughing so hard that tears came to his eyes. When he could finally control himself, he explained the story to Vuillaume, who also became convulsed with laughter. Hart, puzzled by all this, sat in stony silence, seemingly unconcerned that he was out of things. He knew that his turn would come because he had the money, and so he was content to wait.

"Your Italian," Tarisio asked Lott, "where did you learn to speak it?"

Lott went on with his story. The Adelphi, finally caught up in a slack season, closed down. The orchestra conductor had bought a female elephant and decided to exhibit her throughout the British Empire. In the meantime he had discovered Lott's hoax, and as an insult had offered the violinmaker a job as the elephant's attendant. Much to his chagrin, Lott accepted the job.

"A man has to eat," Lott explained to Tarisio. "And John Lott was never above honest work, even if it meant tending an elephant." So he went on a tour with the animal. The elephant's trainer was an Italian who addressed the elephant in that tongue, and Lott heard so much of it that eventually he learned enough to speak it.

At last Tarisio mopped his brow and took command of the situation. That was the start of the strangest violin transaction he had ever engaged in. He conversed with Vuillaume in French, with Lott in Italian, and the latter with Hart in English.

The two Englishmen remained in Paris for a week, and eventually the language barrier was overcome to the point where Tarisio could understand Lott's cockney accent and

Hart could understand Tarisio's English. Hart acquired a number of fine Cremona violins, Vuillaume a good commission on the deal, and Tarisio made two British friends.

During the week all four men visited the opera house, and Tarisio for the first time heard the music of Liszt and Chopin, as well as the voice of Maria Malibran, the operatic idol of France. It was one of the happiest weeks in his life and he was sorry to see it end. But the time had come to prepare for his trip to Spain.

*Crests of Amati, Guarneri, and Stradivari*

*Opera house in Paris, about 1840*

# CHAPTER 20

V UILLAUME'S VERSATILITY and vigor amazed Tarisio.
The Frenchman not only made and repaired violins,
but he was also constantly experimenting, and at that
very moment was at work on ideas for modifying the bow,
the magic wand of violinists. He had been collaborating
with Francis Tourte, the world's foremost craftsman in
bow-making. Although this genius could neither read nor
write, he commanded enormous prices for his bows, often
more than Tarisio was getting for some of his Cremona
violins.

Although Vuillaume had promised to introduce Tarisio
to the old man, other things had intervened to prevent
the meeting. But they had a chance to discuss the subject
the night before he left for Spain, and in the course of
several hours he received a complete education on the art
of bow-making.

Tourte had accidentally discovered that Pernambuco
wood, imported from South America and used in France
for industrial dyeing purposes, made the most satisfactory
bows. Because this wood was nearly always knotty,

cracked, and crooked, Tourte often had to search through eight to ten tons of it before finding a few pieces with a straight grain suitable for a violin bow. This was one of the reasons, Vuillaume told Tarisio, why Tourte got so much money for his sticks. It was not unusual for Tourte to be paid as much as five hundred francs for one.

In his own field, Vuillaume went on, Tourte was as great a master as Stradivari. He gave the most minute attention to the hair he used, preferring French horsehair to that of any other country because he felt it was larger and stronger. Assisted by his daughter, who was continually occupied by sorting the hairs and selecting the longest and best, Tourte would first scour the hair with soap. Then he soaked it in bran water and finally, after removing foreign matter, he plunged it into pure water lightly colored with blueing. When the strands had dried, Tourte would use approximately two hundred hairs to assemble his bow.

"So tedious a task as counting horsehairs would drive me to distraction," Tarisio commented. "How could Tourte retain his sanity?"

Vuillaume laughed. "Francis Tourte is an astounding person. How a man without any instruction, unable to read or write a word, could, from instinct alone, become so marvelous a craftsman seems beyond comprehension."

Vuillaume then told Tarisio about his pet project—finding a scientific explanation for the sound-producing action of the bow on the violin string.

"Perhaps," he said wistfully, "the world will not remember Vuillaume as a violinmaker, but as a scientist."

He had first become curious about bows when he noticed that, although a bow on a string would not stop it from vibrating, the touch of a finger would.

"Tourte and I decided that it is the continued action

of the bow on the string that produces the result. When a bow is drawn across the string, it creates a series of very rapid shocks which are so regular that they maintain the vibration of the string instead of destroying it. This phenomenon, we found, was affected not only by the elasticity of the hair, but by the rosin with which we coated it."

"But how did you arrive at the exact dimensions of the bow-stick itself?" Tarisio asked.

"Mathematics," Vuillaume replied. "Complicated mathematics. Eventually we arrived at an exact formula to make the perfectly balanced stick."

Tarisio threw up his hands. "Spare me the details," he protested. "I am confused enough as it is. I shall stick to violins and leave the bows to greater minds than mine."

When he traveled to Le Havre the next day to board a ship for Spain, he thought of Tourte and regretted missing the opportunity to meet him; for by now he had lost all sense of shyness before important people, and hungered to know them.

The voyage across the Bay of Biscay was pleasant, and Tarisio found that some of his old eagerness to search for Cremonas had returned. He could scarcely wait until his ship docked.

He liked his first glimpse of Spain because it was warm and sunny, and reminded him of the country around Milan. Life was leisurely and the people were like those around Fontanetto. He easily found Ortego's shop, a small cubbyhole facing a market place.

The Madrid violinmaker was a squat, swarthy man with a reputation for curtness and a thoroughly unjustified regard for his own abilities. Violin men in Paris and London, for example, referred to him as a butcher; Tarisio was not surprised when he found himself almost totally ignored.

Ortego, he knew, was the kind of man who boasted of undoing the bungling of others; in other words, a man who masqueraded his vandalism under the name of legitimate business. Flattery was indicated, Tarisio thought, and so, after introducing himself, he said: "I have heard about you, Señor Ortego, especially your work in making Stradivari instruments playable."

The surly Spaniard unbent. Spitting a stream of tobacco at the wall, he remarked drily: "Stradivari? Bah! His varnish? Good, but his fiddles—" He shrugged. Earlier in the year, he said proudly, a young woman had come in with a Stradivari cello. She had paid a good price for it, too, but the tone was terrible. It croaked like a bullfrog. But he had quickly diagnosed the trouble. The top was no good, and neither was the bass-bar. So what did Ortego do to remedy the situation? He simply made a top of his own, plus a new bass-bar, and presto—the cello had a voice again!

Although he was already familiar with the story, the Spaniard's way of telling it left Tarisio aghast and disgusted. Ortego's top, if he ever got his hands on it, would go to a toothpick maker. He cleared his throat as if to speak, but the Spaniard anticipated him. So Tarisio would like to know the name of the lady with the cello? There had been a Frenchman in some time ago and he, too, wanted the lady's name. But Ortego wouldn't tell him, and could not see why he should accommodate Tarisio, either.

A hundred-franc note suddenly appeared on the bench beside the Spaniard. He put down his tools, picked up the banknote, examined it carefully in the light, and for the first time looked Tarisio directly in the eyes. Tarisio stared back at a swarthy person with heavy eyebrows, sallow features, and a cold, thin mouth.

Ortego made a brief stab at respectability. He never revealed the names of patrons, he said smoothly, the words rolling out like dripping oil. But he was well acquainted in Madrid and knew of only one person who might own a Stradivari cello—the Countess Margaretta Duero.

For his one hundred francs Tarisio also got directions. Ortego sent him to the Cathedral San Isidro El Real, just around the corner in the Calle de Toledo. It was a large granite building that he couldn't possibly miss. Ortego stared rudely at Tarisio, eyeing him up and down. "You are not a Frenchman," he said.

"No," Tarisio replied, "I am not a Frenchman, I am Italian." He turned and strode out the door.

Ortego called after him: "The priest speaks both French and Italian fluently." But Tarisio did not stop.

He found the cathedral easily and had no trouble gaining an immediate audience with the priest, to whom he explained his mission. The cello, Tarisio said, was mutilated by the Madrid violinmaker who had removed the original top and substituted his own work. He had acquired the original top, Tarisio said, but it was of little value without the rest of the instrument, and, likewise, the cello was of no value without its original top. If he could restore all of the original parts, the cello would be quite valuable.

The priest nodded. "I am aware of that," he said. "In fact, I attempted to dissuade the Countess when I first learned that she contemplated this project, but to no avail. The Countess is a strong-willed young lady."

He consulted his watch. That evening at eight, he said,

the Countess was having a small reception to which he had been invited. He would be delighted to send a note telling her that he was bringing a friend. "Then I shall introduce you properly and you can negotiate with her. But mind you, the Countess Duero is a very vixenish young lady, and she may charm you right out of your last peso."

"We shall see about that," Tarisio laughed. "Meanwhile I will go sightseeing to while away the hours."

The priest raised an admonishing finger. It would be best if Tarisio went back to his hotel to rest, because the afternoon heat in Madrid was unbearable. "We water the sidewalks twice in the afternoon here," he said. "But at nightfall, the cool breeze of the Guadarrama cools the city and all is gay again."

Tarisio decided to take this advice. He went to his hotel to rest, and again presented himself at the cathedral at seven o'clock that evening.

In the carriage beside his host he enjoyed the sights. Madrid was at its loveliest. The sun had just begun to dip behind the distant mountain peaks, and a cloudless sky hovered over the city like a sapphire of flawless beauty. The streets were alive with gay men and women, but despite the crowds there was an orderliness that impressed Tarisio. The carriage turned into the Calle Mayor, rolled through a lofty archway, and entered a large plaza. The priest called Tarisio's attention to the solid wall of buildings that surrounded the plaza.

Lights glittered from many windows. Iron-caged balconies, jutting from each story, clung to the fronts of the structures, and the muffled buzz of many voices floated down in the breeze. It reminded Tarisio of the night sounds of the forests in Italy, alive with muted, indistinguishable stirrings.

"A heavenly place," he sighed.

"It would seem so," the priest said sadly, "but this is one of Madrid's most tragic paradoxes. Here in this plaza hundreds of men and women have gone to their deaths. We are stopping at the very spot where a gallows stood." He pointed to a building a few yards off, the Panaderia, where, he said, the Queen-Mother Mariana and her son once had sat on the balcony from early morning until late at night, watching a parade of unfortunate Jews and heretics taking their last steps into eternity. The plaza had been bathed in blood many times, and although that was many years ago, Madrid had never forgotten. This was a street of nightmares.

The carriage rolled on, and turned into the Calle de Embojadores. It stopped in front of a triumphal arch whose stone and brick towered toward the darkening sky. This was the Puerta de Toledo, the priest said, completed just two days ago and to be dedicated tomorrow.

"Madrid progresses," Tarisio commented.

"I wish that were true," the priest replied. "Four years ago on this very spot the Spanish patriot Rafael Riego was hanged by King Ferdinand. Madrid has composed an anthem to his memory—the hymn of Riego—but only yesterday another man was hanged from this arch, before its mortar had set."

"It seems incredible, Padre, that there could be so much violence in so beautiful a city!"

"I know, but it is true; Madrid is a jealous city. She hides her treasures and her sins from the casual eye. Behind this façade of serenity is a black, black heart."

The carriage drew up in front of a brightly lighted

villa, a large sprawling structure that indicated wealth and authority.

"We are here," the priest said. "And remember—the lady is a charming vixen."

"Good," exclaimed Luigi. "The charm of an intelligent lady is just what I need to crown a most delightful trip!"

As he stepped down the soft strains of stringed music were audible. The affair was a reception for a new hero, the priest explained, adding that in Spain all heroes were matadors. The Countess captured them all, he said, but she was just as likely to have a reception for a poet, a painter, or an architect. She had entertained Francisco Goya a year or two ago, and she would have Churriguera if he were still alive, if only to stand around and explain the baroque design of her villa. "Who knows, she might even entertain for you when she discovers what a celebrity you are!"

The villa was ablaze with light. In one corner young women danced and kept time with castanets while a number of young men looked on admiringly. Here and there small groups sipped drinks and talked, while in an adjoining room tables were occupied by card players. Against a far wall stood a long table loaded with food—everything from *paella* to *faboda*, *goÿpacho* and *cochinillo*.

A young woman walked up. "Padre," she exclaimed, "how delightful to have you!" Her eyes appraised Tarisio briefly.

"Countess," the priest said, "I have the honor to present my friend, Señor Tarisio, of Milan. He collects rare violins."

Tarisio saw a woman in her early thirties. She was petite, dark, and—to him—almost unbelievably beautiful. Her skin was the color of cream. She had blue eyes, a tiny nose, ruby-red lips, and coal-black hair done up in a large silky mass that perched atop her head like a crown. She was exquisitely formed. Dazzled, Tarisio murmured an acknowledgment. The Countess measured him with one split-second glance and took him by the arm. "Come," she said, "I will show you around."

Luigi looked appealingly at the priest, saw only an amused smile on his lips, and protested mildly. "But your guest of honor, Countess, the bullfighter; shouldn't you——"

The woman cut him short with a laugh. "Manuel is much too busy with the young señoritas. Anyway, tonight I am interested more in violins than in matadors."

The priest wagged a finger at her jovially. "Margaretta," he admonished, "I haven't noticed you at confession lately."

"Padre," she replied, glancing quickly at Tarisio, "it is inevitable that you will see me at confession this very week." The pressure on Tarisio's arm tightened. It gave him a feeling of uneasiness, then a thrill foreign to him, and he quickly moved away with his charming captor.

The Countess guided him across the floor, through a heavily draped archway and onto a patio. She gestured him into a chair, filled a glass with wine, and sat down on a stool facing him.

"Now, Señor Tarisio, tell me about yourself."

"I haven't met your husband," he began.

"You won't," she snapped. "He is dead."

Tarisio mumbled his regrets, telling himself that he was a fool, when her next words stung him to surprise.

"My late husband eventually picked an argument with a better pistol shot," she explained. "Any more questions?"

She had command of the situation now, and Tarisio

sighed because it was always that way when he met people. Just when he felt certain that he had the advantage, something always occurred to take it away from him.

"Countess," he began.

She cut him short. "My friends call me Margaretta," she interrupted. "What do they call you, besides 'Tarisio'?"

"My mother calls me Luigi."

"What do your lady friends call you?"

"I only had one. She called me Luigi, too."

There was a bright gleam in the Countess' eyes and a hint of mischief in her voice. "Luigi," she said, "I want you to tell me all about Italy and Cremona violins. After that I am going to show you how wonderful Spain really is. This will be a very special project for me!"

"You have never been to Italy?"

"Of course," she replied gaily. "But I want to see it through your eyes. Tell me about Cremona."

The breeze brought her perfume to life. Her eyes glowed with an amethystine radiance, highlighting the creamy texture of her skin. They were friendly eyes, wide-set, and completely guileless. Tarisio trusted them.

"Cremona," he began, "is like a great yellow rose growing in the desert."

Her laughter was musical and had warmth. "It is not like that at all," she contradicted. "Cremona is flat, dull, and drab. I spent my honeymoon there."

What happened next, Tarisio rationalized later, must have been the chemistry of the occasion. The Countess Duero looked at him, gently lifted her delicate hands up, and Tarisio's face bent down. He had met his woman and he was in love.

A discreet cough broke the silence and the two saw the priest towering in the doorway.

The Countess leaped to her feet. "Padre," she exclaimed, "this Señor Tarisio is a most charming man."

The priest smiled. "Obviously," he remarked, glancing at the Italian's discomfiture, "you have charmed him out of his senses. I have come to rescue him. It is time to leave."

The young woman shook her head. "Padre," she said, looking the black-robed figure straight in the eyes, "I want Señor Tarisio to stay." She faltered a moment and there was a note of humility in her voice when she continued: "We have much to talk about."

The priest glanced at Tarisio. "My son," he said, "the Countess Duero is the most gracious hostess in Madrid. There are the bullfights——"

"And the pigeon shoots, too," the woman interjected quickly.

There was also dancing, and there were old castles to see, museum and art galleries to explore, exquisite shops to visit, filled with beautiful leatherwork, poetry, basket work, the marvelous jewelry of Toledo steel inlaid with gold and gems; there were so many things in Madrid that even the Countess had never seen, and for which she had suddenly acquired a great desire.

Tarisio stayed, and the next few days passed like a delightful dream. Tarisio and his new love talked incessantly and they went everywhere together. The bullfights were first. Tarisio enjoyed the colorful opening parade, the maneuvers of the picadores, the work of the banderillos, but the killing by the matador sickened him. This was not a sport, he thought, as they left the arena one afternoon. It was a sordid ballet of death in a traditional pattern which man and bull must follow.

The couple spent the following days exploring places in

Carrera de San Jerónimo, where the antique shops were filled with rare works of silver and gold and held Tarisio spellbound. They walked through all the little intersecting streets, drinking in the hidden beauty of Madrid which eludes the casual visitor. At noon they spent an hour in one of the cafés.

For Tarisio it was an adventure never to be forgotten, for his companion a dream come true. Tarisio learned this one afternoon as they looked at paintings in the Velásquez room of the Prado, Madrid's magificent museum. They stood before Las Meninas, the painting of the Infanta Margarita María, attended by her maids of honor and two dwarfs. Quite suddenly Luigi put an arm around Margaretta and kissed her. He realized then that he had never been in love before. The Countess Duero was the woman for him and he knew it as well as he knew that they were standing there. "I love you," he said.

The Infanta Margarita María, her dwarfs, and her maids of honor seemed to smile back from their cloistered shelter in paint and canvas. The Countess never moved. She and Tarisio were like a single statue in the silent room. "Darling," he said, "please don't let me go home alone. Come to Italy with me. I love you and I need you. We have the rest of our lives to do all the things we have talked about. Will you marry me?"

A small voice said: "Yes," and when Tarisio looked down into her face he saw tears of joy.

Arm in arm, they walked out into the Plaza de Castelar and down the promenade Paseo del Prado. The heat of the afternoon engulfed them.

The business of the Bass of Spain came up quite accidentally that day. After dinner that evening, as they sat on the patio where they had first become acquainted, Tarisio remarked that he would soon have to return to Paris. The Countess mentioned the cello. She had seen the Padre and he had spoken of Tarisio's quest, so she had made all arrangements for him. An aunt now had the instrument and it would be delivered in the morning. Tarisio could set his own price.

When it was delivered the next day Tarisio was delighted to offer four thousand francs—an offer instantly accepted. The instrument was everything he hoped it would be, except for Ortego's miserable top. Built on the grand pattern, the cello had an elegant scroll. Details of the original top, which was safe in Paris, came to Tarisio's mind, and as he examined this latest treasure he realized how stunning it would be when restored to its original condition. The back was of excellent quality, cut from a beautiful piece of wood, but the ribs had been cut the wrong way of the grain, a rare mistake in Stradivari's work. The varnish was clear and full of fire. Tarisio had seen other fine cellos, but this was the queen of them all; even the error in wood cutting on the ribs seemed to add something to this instrument.

Later that day, on his way to Bilbao for the return voyage to France, Tarisio stopped briefly at San Isidro el Real. "You know, Padre," he said, "I believe this is the very first time in my adult life that I have stopped into a cathedral or church not intending to remove some treasure."

"So?" the priest said. "And aren't you removing one of my treasures?"

Luigi smiled happily. "So you know already?"

The priest nodded.

"As soon as I can complete my business in Paris, in

about a month," Tarisio continued, "I shall return and we will be married. Margaretta wishes you to perform the ceremony, and so do I."

The priest put an arm around Tarisio's shoulder. "Go and return with God's grace," he said.

*A street in old Madrid*

*"Bass of Spain"* courtesy *Carlos Prieto, the present owner*

*"Bass of Spain" courtesy Carlos Prieto, the present owner*

# CHAPTER 21

Tᴀʀɪsɪo ᴛʜᴏᴜɢʜᴛ Bilboa scarcely the kind of city one would enjoy visiting. He disliked its squat buildings and the constant odor of fish that drifted inland from the Bay of Biscay. He also disliked the rancid tang of salt-water air. But he quickly shrugged away his feelings. His coach traveled down the Gran Vía and stopped at its terminus, within sight of the Rio Nervion that flowed north into the Bay of Biscay.

After lunch Tarisio left his cello at the terminal for safe-keeping and walked to the quays to book passage for France. Ships of all types were tied up there—brigs, luggers, a sloop and several topsail schooners—but it was a heavily rigged vessel that drew his attention. Long lines of men were busy loading boxes and crates aboard, and Tarisio decided to inquire there first. He struggled up a gangplank, picked his way along the cluttered deck, and found the skipper to be a pleasant Frenchman.

It would be a slow trip, the skipper warned, taking at least two weeks to Cherbourg. There would be stops en route at Royan and Nantes. Besides, he would not guarantee any degree of comfort. But Tarisio was anxious to leave and the *Excelsior* looked like the safest thing in the river.

"Be aboard by midnight," the captain said at last. "We'll sail any time after that, as soon as the tide is right."

Tarisio paid his fare and hurried off the ship, deciding to kill time with sightseeing in the city.

The afternoon was hot and oppressingly muggy, a prelude to foul weather. Tarisio walked slowly across the bridge of San Anton, stopping in the center to look down upon the traffic in the river. The *Excelsior* was a scene of frenzied activity, and the huge piles of cargo on the quay were diminishing rapidly. In addition to the long lines of men carrying and wheeling cargo, a large net, swinging from a boom, swallowed up huge amounts and deposited them in the fore hatchway. Tarisio watched the activity for a few minutes, then crossed to the right bank of the Nervion and turned into the Arenol, Bilboa's busiest street.

Oxcarts laden with ore trundled toward a smelter at the edge of the city. A south wind, thick with the musty odor of burning oil and molten metal, churned the dusty street. Tarisio coughed, and headed north. He found a small restaurant, ate a leisurely meal, and decided to go back across the city, reclaim his cello and report early to the *Excelsior*. For him there was nothing of interest in Bilboa. As he stepped to the door of the restaurant, the bells on a nearby church tolled the hour of seven. Tarisio consulted his watch, which registered only five o'clock.

Puzzled, he questioned a waiter and learned that his watch was wrong. The bells of Los Santos Juanes were never in error, Tarisio was assured, and all Bilboa paced itself by the chimes. Tarisio thanked his informant, hurried across the bridge and saw that the activity around the *Excelsior* had ceased. She swung gently in the current, her ropes creaking, some of her canvas already in place. The dock was deserted. The piles of cargo were gone.

Thick haze was settling over the city and the flame of the smelters lighted the sky to the south. Tarisio quickened his pace, reclaimed his cello at the coach terminal, and ran back to the river. Three gongs sounded from the *Excelsior;* the ship would sail in the next ten minutes. Tarisio raced through the darkness to the gangplank. The wind had picked up, and the ship tugged at her moorings. At the head of the gangplank, his swarthy face illuminated by the glow of lamps, the mate stood peering down at the quay, shouting to Tarisio to hurry, that they were ready to cast off. Tarisio ran up the gangplank lugging his cello and baggage. The moment he stepped on the deck the order was given to cast off. The lights of the city slid by and faded away in the distance.

The captain grinned broadly when Luigi walked into the deckhouse. "You're lucky," he said. "We had to leave earlier than expected. There's a storm in the offing, and we had to clear the harbor before it starts. When the wind is from the northwest, it's almost impossible to get out."

The rough water began to slap the bottom of the ship, and the captain explained that they had now cleared the harbor and were out in the bay, where the water was rougher. "Is your cello valuable?" he asked then, with a curious glance at the instrument.

"Extremely," Tarisio replied. "It is a Stradivari. It needs restoration, but that is all arranged for." He told the captain the story of the instrument and the latter, who had some slight appreciation of old violins, listened with interest.

"People are strange," he mused. "Always trying to improve on the masters."

A sailor strode into the little cabin, reporting the barometer to be dropping fast. The captain snapped an order to lower some canvas and told Tarisio that the weather was beginning to look worse than expected. The safest place for him and his cello was in a little cabin just behind the bow, in front of the fore hatchway. He beckoned a deckhand and ordered Tarisio taken forward, promising to look in on him from time to time. "And remember," he cautioned, "stay inside and hang onto that cello!"

The wind whistled through the rigging and clouds of spray broke over the side of the ship as Tarisio struggled forward. The vessel rolled and lunged. Encumbered with the cello and his luggage, he had trouble keeping his footing; but finally, after a struggle that left him winded and soaked to the skin, he reached the shelter of the little cabin and secured the door. He took a small flint gun from the wall and in a moment had two oil lamps burning. There was nothing in the cabin except a single bunk, a chair, and several large coils of rope. He put the cello down on the deck and stretched out on the bunk to wait out the storm.

He could feel the movement of the ship as it rose to the top of a big wave and then pitched forward, leaving him gasping for breath. The wind was rising steadily, howling through the rigging. Suddenly there was a rending noise. The ship jerked violently sideways and the cello slid across the deck, crashing into a bulkhead. Tarisio leaped from the bunk and stripped off the canvas covering. At the last second, the cello had flipped over on its side and crashed into a small iron capstan in the bulkhead, shattering Ortego's top. Luigi stripped the thin mattress off his bunk, wrapped it around his treasure, and lashed it together with the rope. Then he tied the bundle to the deck, twisting the rope tightly around the bunk feet which were securely bolted down. Then he returned to his bunk and tried to sleep.

It was daybreak when a member of the crew came in and roused him. The captain wanted his passenger aft. Tarisio followed the sailor back, noting that there was no sight of land anywhere. He had thought the vessel intended to follow the coast to Royan, and had made up his mind to debark there and finish his trip by coach; but the *Excelsior* was miles off course, and at the moment almost due south of Brest. There would be no stop at Royan or Nantes harbor.

At breakfast the captain explained to Tarisio that during the night the storm had reached near-hurricane proportions and part of the cargo had shifted; some of it was smashed. Tarisio realized that only his foresight had saved his precious cello from destruction.

He spent the next two days and nights in the stern with the captain. The wind died down, but a blinding, lashing rainstorm moved in on the hapless ship.

On the morning of the third day a crewman brought news: Brest was dead ahead. Late that evening the *Excelsior* slipped into quiet waters, and the sudden silence roused Tarisio from his sleep. He found the captain busy at the tiller.

"Now what?" he asked.

"It's all over," the skipper replied. "We're in the harbor. There are the lights of Cherbourg. We'll tie up in about two hours. By the way, one of the men checked your cello. It's safe and sound. Hasn't budged an inch from where you lashed it."

By the time the *Excelsior* had docked, Tarisio was ready to step ashore. He learned that he had almost three hours to wait before he could leave for Paris, and decided to spend the time outfitting himself. He smiled ruefully as he examined his clothing. His suit and shoes had been ruined by their treatment on the ship, and he needed the services of a barber. Within a short time he was a new man, shaved, newly clothed, and as neat as though he had just stepped out of his own home.

When he arrived at Vuillaume's home later that day, proudly carrying the Bass of Spain, he was pleased beyond measure at his host's excitement. The cello had suffered no damage except to Ortego's top, and this would soon be discarded. "Let's work on this now," Vuillaume suggested.

Tarisio was delighted. Vuillaume set the instrument on its back and picked up a flat-bladed knife. Probing the varnish at the side of Ortego's top, he found a soft section and pushed the blade in. Then he slowly moved it from side to side. Within ten minutes half of the top was loose from the ribs. "Now this is the tricky part," Vuillaume explained. "You have to get the rest off without splintering any of the ribbing. Watch."

He moved the knife slowly around to the tail button, held it firmly with one hand, then with the other gently pressed the edge of the top. There was a sharp crack, and a section nearly a foot long sprung clear. He repeated the process several times, and in a few more minutes triumphantly lifted off Ortego's top, exposing the interior of the instrument.

Tarisio read the label aloud: "Antonio Stradivari, Cremona, 1701." Then, pointing to the end blocks and ribbing, he cried: "Have you ever seen such wonderful work?" Each block had been fitted into the corners so perfectly that the whole gave the impression of having been moulded from a single piece.

Vuillaume took a small blade and carefully chipped off the remaining glue which had adhered to the top of the ribbing. Then he set the original top temporarily in place. The change in the appearance of the instrument was startling.

"Absolutely magnificent," Vuillaume exclaimed. "And to think that anyone would attempt to replace it! Just think—if Chanot hadn't by the merest chance passed that fellow's shop and noticed this, and if there weren't a man with your persistence, this treasure would have been lost forever!" He removed Stradivari's top, brushed fresh glue around the ribbing, and reset the top, which fell into place so easily that it fitted like the glove on a hand. Then he adjusted holding clamps. The entire procedure had taken a little more than an hour, and when the last clamp was in place Vuillaume remarked: "We'll let it harden all night, and I'll remove the clamps tomorrow."

Tarisio stared happily at the instrument. Vuillaume had done the restoration so remarkably that only an expert could have told that the Bass of Spain had ever been tampered with. A sudden recollection made him blanch. "I have just remembered," he cried in anguish. "The bassbar. Chanot's letter said it was loose."

Vuillaume grinned. "It was," he replied. Then he explained. A small section at the tip had become loose, and when the instrument was played, the vibration caused it to have a rasping sound. "That's undoubtedly what the Countess complained about when she took it to Ortego in the first place," the Frenchman said. "All it ever needed was a few drops of glue. I took care of that the day you left the top here."

Tarisio was relieved. The incident set him to reminiscing. This had not been the first time that he had seen vandalism committed against a work of art. About a year earlier, he said, he had run across a fine Stradivari violin that someone had painted with several coats of red paint. "I found it on a farm," he said. "The workmanship was marvelous, but, alas, some monstrous person had painted it. It was ruined beyond salvage. All that gorgeous varnish—obliterated forever." The sight had so sickened him, he said, that he had left the instrument where it was, although it could have been his for a few francs.

It did not take the Vuillaumes long to discover Tarisio was in love. They pressed him for details, and Luigi was delighted to oblige. But Vuillaume had important news too. He had been conducting experiments on violins with the French acoustical scientist, Felix Savart, and as a result had succeeded in making a duplicate of Paganini's Guarneri so exact that even the great maestro had difficulty in distinguishing between the original and the imitation.

To Tarisio this seemed incredible. "Forgive me, my friend," he said, "but I find this almost impossible to believe."

Madame Vuillaume, who had been listening to the conversation, nodded in confirmation.

Vuillaume reminded Tarisio of the day Paganini had rushed to his home complaining that his violin had lost its voice, and had given him just three days to repair it. "That was when I began to make my copy," Vuillaume said. "As soon as I had removed the top of Paganini's

*Paganini's Joseph Guarnerius*

*Nicolo Paganini*

Guarneri I resolved to analyze the instrument in every part and to create one exactly like it in appearance and tone. I had some wood of first-rate quality, and out of it I got a back and belly that had the same figure in the maple and identical grain of the spruce.

"While you were in Spain I completed the violin and went to Paganini's house. He was practicing at the time, but upon seeing me, he laid his Guarneri on a table. I removed my copy from its case and put it beside the genuine Cremona. Paganini stared at it unbelievingly. He walked around the table looking at both instruments, changed their places, and acted like a man dumbfounded."

"Then what happened?" Tarisio urged.

"Many times," Vuillaume went on, "he picked up the copy, saying that it was the genuine Guarneri. Finally he could stand it no longer. He seized his bow and began to play. Finally he exclaimed: 'They are alike! Whichever is the copy—it has the same tone and the same quality. They are both mine!'"

Vuillaume finally showed Paganini the difference between the two instruments. The genuine Cremona was lighter than the copy he had made and he demonstrated this to Paganini by having him hold both instruments in his hands at the same time, comparing their weight. The older violin would seem a little lighter, he went on, because the natural juices in the wood had long since vanished. Then there was another difference. The telltale little band of clouded wood to be found in the center of most of Joseph's work was missing from the copy, but clearly visible in the genuine Guarneri. The maestro was satisfied with the explanation, but still incredulous at Vuillaume's skill.

"What happened to your violin?" Tarisio asked.

Vuillaume beamed with pride. "I heard today," he replied, "that Paganini has insisted that his one and only pupil, the young artist Ernesto Camillo Sivori, use it exclusively."

A short time later Paganini had come to Vuillaume and offered him five hundred francs if he would make still another copy.

"And will you do it?" Tarisio asked.

Vuillaume shrugged. "I already have attempted it," he said, "but something is lacking; it does not have the tone."

"You thought that you had finally discovered the lost secret of Cremona," Tarisio said gently, "and then, when you felt success within your grasp, you learned that the secret had eluded you!"

Vuillaume nodded, and said that it must have been largely luck that the first copy had turned out so well. Then he told Tarisio of his experiments with Professor Savart, who had just concluded a series of lectures on experimental philosophy at the College of France. Vuillaume had taken a number of Stradivaris and Guarneris to Savart for examination. He had also persuaded Chanot to lend his dismantled instruments to the scientist.

"Professor Savart found that the same sounds were always produced by the same causes, the same forms, and the same proportions. He found, in general terms, that Stradivari's instruments owed their qualities of tone to the excellent choice of wood, the relationship of sonority among the various pieces of wood which compose the instruments, the capaciousness of the belly, the proportions of thickness in top and back, the precision in workmanship, and lastly to the varnish. The latter, incidentally, he told me, protects the wood against the influence of changes of the atmosphere, without offering any obstacle to the elasticity on which the freedom of vibration depends. In other words, the varnish is something out of the ordinary."

Tarisio's face was solemn. "This is most profound," he admitted, "but wouldn't it be much more to the point merely to say that God guided Stradivari's hand? He knew nothing of the science of acoustics."

The professor's experiments were useful, Tarisio admitted, but solved nothing. He once had met a violinmaker who had applied the principles of vibration and had constructed a violin out of some metal. "You should have heard it," he laughed. "The poor fellow spent two years on it. To sum up everything your experiments proved, all you have discovered is that the maple in a Stradivari back is exactly a tone lower than that in a spruce top, and that there is an affinity between them.

"Stradivari knew that one hundred years ago. Do you suppose science will ever be able to explain the affinity of these two tones, not only for each other, but for the human ear as well?"

There was no reply from Vuillaume.

*Announcement for a Vuillaume exhibit*

*Violoncello, viola, and violin, all by Stradivari*

# CHAPTER 22

WORD THAT TARISIO had brought the Bass of Spain to Paris spread mysteriously, and within a day or two scores of Parisian enthusiasts had come to Vuillaume's place to see and admire it. It was then, during a lull in the coming and going of people who had been examining the restored cello, that Tarisio dropped his bombshell.

Tarisio intended to retire. He told Vuillaume that he would go back to Milan, and upon his return bring Le Messie and all his other Cremonas. Then he would give up his wanderings and marry.

"You should see her," he said softly. "A face like a cameo. Her voice is like a tiny bell, clear, bright, and gentle. And when she looks at me, Vuillaume, it is like gazing into the bluest pool one ever saw, deep and clear, reflecting a cloudless sky!"

Madame Vuillaume had stepped into the room in time to hear the end of Tarisio's rhapsody. "And in addition she is a Countess—and the niece of the woman who owned the Bass of Spain! How romantic it all sounds!"

"Yes," Luigi nodded. "When I reached Madrid and

learned that the cello was owned by a Spanish countess,
I expected to deal with a fat, smooth, condescending
woman who would let me know, in a hundred ways, that
she was my superior. And instead I met the most wonderful woman in the world!"

"She must be extraordinary. Any woman would have to
be to compete with Le Messie and your Cremonas," Vuillaume commented drily.

A servant appeared at the door to announce that Aldric
had arrived unexpectedly. Vuillaume and Tarisio exchanged glances.

"News gets around," Vuillaume commented.

Impeccably dressed, Aldric was ushered into the room.
He greeted his hosts, and especially Tarisio, with marked
enthusiasm. Vuillaume was gracious as he motioned his
guest to a chair. He realized that Aldric must have heard
about his acquisition of the Bass of Spain, and sensed that
his visitor was desperate to buy. Here was a chance, he
thought, to make him pay through the nose; for Vuillaume,
despite his own success, envied Aldric's clientele, which
consisted of wealthy patrons of music and members of
royalty all over Europe. Aldric must have a buyer for the
cello and an anxious one, he thought.

"The Bass of Spain is not mine to sell," he said a moment later in response to a direct question. "It belongs to
our friend here, and Tarisio does not desire to sell."

Aldric turned to Luigi abruptly. "Is this true, Tarisio?"

Tarisio nodded. "I am not ready to discuss a sale, M.
Aldric—at least not at present. This Bass of Spain is a very
unusual instrument, and I have not had it long enough to
fully appreciate its value."

"I'll pay twenty thousand francs," Aldric said. "Sight
unseen."

Tarisio opened his mouth to speak, but Vuillaume anticipated him. "Calm yourself, M. Aldric," he said. "First let us show you the Bass of Spain, and then we can discuss the matter further. You see," he said conciliatingly, "while Tarisio owns this instrument, I have a sort of vested interest in it because Tarisio has entrusted to me the task of restoring it. But come, you shall see it for yourself."

The three walked upstairs to Vuillaume's workshop and Aldric hurried over to the instrument. It was smothered beneath dozens of clamps. He scarcely glanced at the sides and bottom of the cello, but peered closely at the top. When he had finished his inspection, he turned to Vuillaume. "Just one question: did you reglue the bass-bar?"

Tarisio cut in. "You seem to know a great deal about this instrument," he remarked. "How did you know that the bass-bar needed gluing?"

Aldric had no choice but to tell all. He had been on the trail of the Bass of Spain for several years because one of his patrons, whose identity he could not reveal, had long tried to buy it from a certain lady in Madrid; Tarisio had beaten him to the instrument by a day. Aldric had met Chanot some time earlier and learned that Tarisio had the top and that all that was wrong with it was the loose bass-bar. Then he had hurried to Spain, but too late. "I must have it, and money is no object," he concluded reluctantly.

Tarisio wondered how high the man would go; he felt that fifty thousand francs was somewhere near Aldric's limit. He was astonished to hear the connoisseur say:

"Would you consider seventy-five thousand francs?"

It was a fantastic offer, and it left Tarisio speechless.

Vuillaume took Aldric gently by the arm. "Let us go back downstairs," he suggested. "There we can discuss the matter in more pleasant surroundings." He knew now that something was wrong, that Aldric needed the instrument so desperately that it was almost a matter of life and death. Downstairs Vuillaume ordered coffee and the three men sat down. "M. Aldric," Vuillaume began, "how long have we known each other?"

"Fifteen, sixteen years."

"And have we been friends?"

Aldric looked at him helplessly and did not reply.

"Well, have we been friends?" Vuillaume insisted.

Aldric shook his head. There was misery in his face.

"That being the case," Vuillaume went on remorselessly, "why should we now give you the opportunity to acquire this treasure? There were many times when you could have helped me, many times when you had many more patrons than instruments to supply them with—when you could have sent some of that patronage my way. And when Tarisio first came to Paris, who was it who gave out the interview about acquiring the Cremonas, an interview that cast doubt upon Tarisio's honesty?"

Aldric bowed his head. What could he say? These things were true. He had behaved abominably. Then a wild expression came into his eyes. "The Bass of Spain," he cried. "I must have it or I am ruined!"

At last the story came out. Aldric had accepted a large advance from a royal patron, and he must now produce the instrument or go to prison.

Tarisio walked to a window and stared at the traffic outside. Then he turned around and said: "M. Aldric, the Bass of Spain is yours for one hundred thousand francs!"

Vuillaume stifled a gasp.

Aldric sat like a man stricken. When he finally gained

his voice, it croaked like a frog's: "My God—one hundred thousand francs?"

Tarisio stood quietly, his arms folded across his chest. "Vuillaume removes the clamps tomorrow," he said briefly, "and then it is yours."

Contorted with emotion, Aldric arose. "I shall be here at nine o'clock," he said. "With the money." His voice was shaky.

No one accompanied him to the door. Vuillaume and Tarisio stood there, abstractedly watching as the once-elegant figure slouched away. All three knew that the man would be ruined, but neither Tarisio nor Vuillaume seemed to feel great joy over Tarisio's revenge.

Late that evening, Tarisio sat down to write his beloved. As he began to compose the letter, his thoughts went back to the days when he could scarcely read or write, when he was clothed in the crudest of cloth, and his meals were infrequent. Now the luxury of his friend's house seemed like his natural habitat. He wrote with bold, broad strokes in the manner of one in whose mind there was no doubt about what he should say.

Promptly at nine o'clock the next morning, Aldric appeared at Vuillaume's place. There were dark circles beneath his eyes. While Tarisio counted the money, he wondered idly where Aldric had managed to raise so much cash during the night. Then he wrote a bill of sale for the Bass of Spain and handed it to Aldric. The thing that occurred next was as unexplainable as the secret of Cremona itself. Aldric had paid his money and was on his way out when Tarisio, suddenly shaking as though he suffered from a fever, called him back. Without preliminary, he counted out eighty thousand francs, and, as Vuillaume watched him in complete disbelief, Tarisio shoved the

*Antonius Stradivarius, Cremona 1693*

*The Harrison, owned by Kyung-Wha Chung*

money into the hands of the stunned Aldric. "I cannot accept a sou more than twenty thousand francs," Luigi said, and abruptly turned away.

Like a man in a trance, rescued from the brink of bankruptcy, Aldric left Vuillaume's house with his cello, his reputation, and his sanity. Tarisio never saw him again.

What had prompted this act of generosity? Conscience? An innate sense of justice? Pity? Long after Aldric had left Tarisio struggled to explain his actions, but to no avail. All he could do was shrug his shoulders in a gesture of helplessness.

But Paris was to hear of his magnanimous gesture; Vuillaume saw to that.

# CHAPTER 23

THE DEVASTATING NEWS hit Tarisio as though he had been struck by lightning. Madame Vuillaume had brought in a letter, and Tarisio, seeing that it came from the Sacredote of San Isidro in Madrid, ripped it open with trembling fingers. He read the first paragraph, then the letter slid from his fingers and fluttered to the floor. Wordlessly, like a man in a trance, he walked out of the room.

Madame Vuillaume picked up the letter, glanced quickly at it and gasped: "Jean Baptiste, this is horrible!" Vuillaume came to her side, and together they read the priest's letter:

My dear Tarisio:
It is with grieving heart that I perform the sad task of informing you of the tragedy to the Countess Margaretta Duero. She is no longer with us.
Yesterday morning, after having spent several hours in my study making the marriage arrangements and talking of you, she stepped into the Calle de Toledo in front of the Cathedral—and into the path of a runaway team. I loved her as though she had been my child, and I tell you as I have told myself that this is Christ's will, and that He has taken

*Joseph Guarnerius, filius Andrea, Cremona 1706*

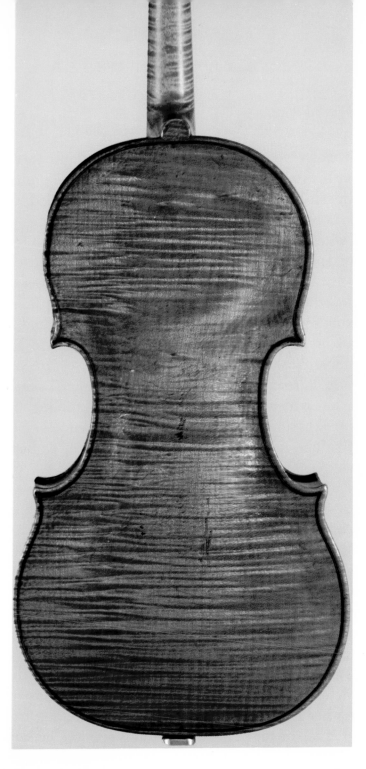

*ex-Paganini*

her to His bosom. I shall pray for you as for her. Conquiescat in Pace.

Father Anthony

It was several days before Tarisio was able to venture
from his room to make some pretense of going about his
business. Vuillaume, meanwhile, had been called to Brussels on business by his brother, N. F. Vuillaume, and upon
his wife had fallen the burden of rousing Tarisio from his
grief and lethargy. On the third day after word of Margaretta's death, Madame Vuillaume decided on a new
tack, other methods of rousing Tarisio having failed. Selecting several of her husband's newest violins and several
bows he had made, she carried them upstairs to Tarisio's
room, and asked him for his help.

"My husband is no longer a young man," she began.
"He has pursued a dual career for years, building and selling violins and bows. Now I think he should confine himself to one or the other—either make them or become a
dealer."

Tarisio nodded. "I agree with you. One is either a maker
or a seller, but not both; for in each there is art enough
for any man."

"I have some samples of his work," Madame Vuillaume
went on. "I know you have seen them before, but I ask
you now, as our friend, to examine them with the same
discrimination and astuteness as you would a Cremona.
Tell me, in your opinion, will Jean Baptiste ever be considered a truly great maker?"

Tarisio long ago had formed an opinion about that, but
in deference to his hostess he took one of the instruments
from her hands and subjected it to a searching examination. Then he faced her again. In his opinion, he said, only

the test of time could be used to measure Jean Baptiste Vuillaume.

"His work?" Tarisio said. "It is wonderful. But your husband is a copyist, not a creator. I wonder as I hold this violin—a gorgeous re-creation of one of Stradivari's finest models—whether it has instilled in it the soul of a genius? Has Vuillaume taken a bit of himself and intermingled it with the ingredients of wood, varnish, and glue? I have often asked myself whether Vuillaume will someday occupy a niche beside the Amatis, the Stradivaris, the Guarneris, and Bergonzi. In my heart I don't believe so. This, my dear friend, is my opinion, but only time can give a conclusive answer."

*Efrem Zimbalist holding a Vuillaume violin*

*Petrus Guarnerius, Mantua 1707*

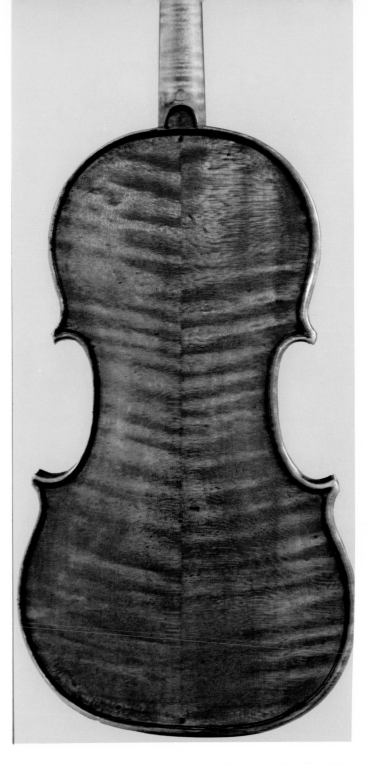

*owned by Earl Carlyss of Juilliard Quartet*

*Gaspard Duiffoprugcar*

# CHAPTER 24

J EAN BAPTISTE VUILLAUME had long nursed a secret ambition, and he revealed it one evening while Tarisio
admired one of his friend's most prized possessions—a
superb bass-viol made in 1510 by Gaspard Duiffoprugcar.
Duiffoprugcar had made this instrument for Francis I,
King of France. After passing through various hands, it
was finally acquired by J. M. Raoul, King's Counsellor
and Advocate in the Court of Cassation, and when Raoul
died, Vuillaume had bought it from the estate.

Tarisio admired the instrument and Vuillaume discussed
its history, pointing out that Duiffoprugcar probably was
the forerunner of the Italian school of violinmaking. Vuillaume had been so enchanted with his curio that he had
made a study of the history of stringed instruments, and
Tarisio was impressed with the extent of Vuillaume's
knowledge. Then Vuillaume confided his secret ambition
to his friend: he wanted, someday, to be known not only
as a maker and dealer of violins and bows, but as an historian as well. Since he had known Tarisio, he said, he had

*Joseph Guarnerius del Gesu, Cremona 1729*

*ex-Balokovic owned by Erick Friedman*

learned a great deal about the Cremona School but there were still gaps in his notes.

"We could go to Cremona together," Tarisio suggested, "and I will take you around. I will show you where Stradivari worked and died, where the Guarneris worked, the home of the Bergonzis; and now, since old Bergonzi is dead, I will take you to see Enrico Ceruti, the last living link between the Cremona of today and the Cremona of Stradivari's time."

The idea for Vuillaume's trip to Italy was born that simply. Both he and Tarisio put aside all their business affairs, and spent almost three months in and around Cremona. They delved into the history of the Amati family, and compiled a long list of makers who had learned their trade from the Amatis: Joseph Guarneri of Cremona, who worked from 1680 to 1710; Florinus Florentus of Bologna, 1685 to 1715; Francis Rugger, or Ruggieri, 1670 to 1720; Peter Guarneri, brother of Joseph and second son of Andrew, 1690 to 1720; John Grancino, son of Paolo, of Milan, 1696 to 1720; John Baptiste Grancino, brother of John, of Milan, 1690 to 1700; Alexander Mezzadie, of Ferrara, 1690 to 1720; Vincent Rugger, of Cremona, 1700 to 1730; Giovanni Battista Rogeri, of Brescia, 1700 to 1725; his son Pietro Rogeri, of Brescia, 1710 to 1720; Gaetano Pasta, of Brescia, 1710 to 1740; Francis Grancino, son of John and grandson of Paolo, of Milan, 1710 to 1746; Peter Guarneri, son of Joseph and grandson of Andrew, of Cremona, 1725 to 1740; Santo Seraphino of Venice, 1730 to 1745; and the fabulous Stradivari.

But they hunted in vain for some record of the birth of Stradivari, although a search through a catalogue of ancient families who had held public office in Cremona revealed many interesting facts. Various Stradivaris had been living in Cremona since 1127. Tarisio found an entry for Ottolinus Stradivari, a senator patriae, in 1127. Another Stradivari, Egidius, had been a senator in 1186. By 1429, the two discovered, the family appeared to have changed its name somewhat; Tarisio and Vuillaume found the record of Guglielmus Stradivertus, a lawyer who died in 1439. They searched records in the Church of St. Laurence of the Olivite Fathers and the Church of St. Andrew for mention of Antonio Stradivari, but in vain.

One day Tarisio had an idea. He took Vuillaume to see Father Julius Fusetti, Vicar of the Cathedral of Cremona, who had taken a liking to Luigi and in whom the young man had often confided.

Many of Cremona's churches had been suppressed in the past, Father Fusetti said, and more often than not their archives stolen, concealed, or destroyed. He himself had hunted vainly for some evidence of Stradivari's age.

"There is only one place in the world that I know of where you will find a record of it," he said, "and you yourself have access to it."

The look of astonishment on Tarisio's face abruptly cleared. "Of course!" he cried to Vuillaume. "Here we are ransacking Cremona for evidence of Stradivari's birth, when all the time it is right in Paris!"

Vuillaume stared at his friend, uncomprehending. Tarisio explained. He had just remembered that one of the violins that he had bought from Di Salabue had a peculiarity on the label, which bore the date of 1736. Stradivari, undoubtedly proud of his skill at his advanced age, penned a notation on that label in his own hand, stating that he was ninety-two years old at the time. That would definitely set his birth in the year 1644. Furthermore, Tarisio

*Sanctus Seraphin, Venice 1740*

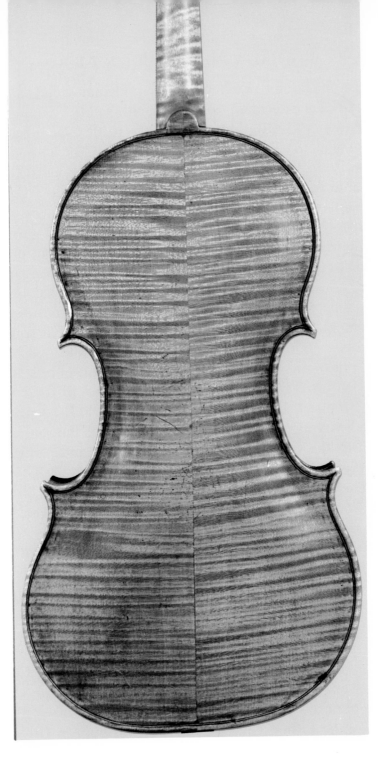

*owned by Zino Francescatti*

went on, he and Vuillaume had sold that violin, an unusually fine specimen, to their friend Gand.

Father Fusetti added importance to that label by telling them that in response to their requests he had circularized all the churches in that part of Italy, asking them to hunt for data on Stradivari. But nowhere, he said, was there any birth record, although marriage records of his parents had been uncovered.

In 1644, Father Fusetti went on, the bubonic plague had swept through Cremona and its environs, taking many lives. Therefore it was reasonable to assume that Stradivari's parents had fled to some distant city, returning to Cremona after the plague had subsided, and that Antonio had been born during their self-imposed exile.

Tarisio and Vuillaume had made several efforts to see Enrico Ceruti, and one day, near the end of their visit, they found him in his shop. Now that Carlo Bergonzi was dead, Ceruti, whom Tarisio knew well, was the sole living link to the Cremona of Stradivari's time, and Vuillaume was anxious to meet him.

Their visit was cordial, but Ceruti could add little to Vuillaume's research on Stradivari. He did, however, have interesting data on his own background.

When Lorenzo Storioni—who as a young man had known Stradivari, Guarneri, and Carlo Bergonzi intimately —decided to retire, he sold his business to Ceruti's grandfather, Giovanni Battista Ceruti. That was in 1790, just nine years before Storioni died. Storioni's successor was thirty-five years old.

"Grandfather favored the Amati pattern," young Ceruti went on. "And when he died in 1817 he had made about five hundred violins and cellos."

Ceruti's father, Giuseppe Ceruti, was born in Cremona

in 1787, but he was more a restorer than a creator. "Even today," Ceruti said, "he still likes to tinker, but he's too old to work. The business is all mine."

Young Ceruti astonished Vuillaume and Tarisio with an account of his own production. Despite the fact that he had a very large repair business, he already had turned out nearly three hundred instruments.

Near the end of their talk Ceruti asked Tarisio a question: "Do you ever run across my grandfather's violins? And how are they regarded?"

Truthful and to the point as usual, Tarisio replied: "Quite often. They are fine instruments, but they will never rank with those of Amati, Stradivari, Guarneri, or Bergonzi."

Their talk with Ceruti was the climax of their visit and by the time they returned to Paris, Vuillaume was the best-informed man in Europe on Cremona's great violin-makers. But he never got around to realizing his ambition to become an historian because too many other things intervened. When his information was finally put into print it was only part of a book written by his friend François Fetis, Director of the Conservatory of Music in Brussels.

*Joseph Guarnerius del Gesu, Cremona 1734*

*owned by Pinchas Zukerman*

*Violin by Enrico Ceruti, 1852*

# CHAPTER 25

THE INFLUENCE EXERTED upon each other by Charles Reade, the English author, and Luigi Tarisio, is almost beyond measure. Tarisio inspired Reade to some of his most widely read and quoted writings, the "Letters to the Pall Mall Gazette," and through Reade Tarisio was able to send hundreds of Cremona violins into the world of art and music.

They met at Vuillaume's place after Tarisio and the Frenchman returned from Italy, and their liking for each other was instantaneous and lasting despite their great differences in personality. Reade was poised, sarcastic, and snobbish. In his dress and manner he was correct almost to a fault. Tarisio, on the other hand, was the direct opposite. Moreover, there was a basic difference in their philosophy of life. This was especially true when it touched the subject of violins.

Tarisio believed that the violins of Stradivari and his contemporaries were made to be played upon for the enjoyment of mankind; whereas Reade believed that these instruments were too precious to be in the hands of any

*Francesco Ruggeri, Cremona 1690*

except the greatest artists, and, since there were never more than a handful of these at any one time, that the instruments should be preserved in museums. It was a subject upon which they were never able to agree. But this fundamental difference, instead of dividing them, merely brought them closer, for after all other subjects of conversation had been exhausted, they always had this absorbing one to return to.

To illustrate his point that amateurs were a menace to the preservation of fine old instruments, Reade cited several instances where he had seen violins on which the varnish had been nicked and badly worn by careless handling. But Tarisio shrugged this off, maintaining that he himself had handled many which had been neglected and exposed to great changes in temperature and humidity, whose varnish not only had survived this, but still retained its beauty.

Once Vuillaume, who had been sitting by quietly listening to the conversation, took a hand himself when the subject turned to varnish; and since he was unable to converse with Reade in English, he addressed his remarks to Tarisio. Reade should hear Tarisio's theory about Stradivari's varnish, he said, because Reade, being an expert on old violins, might have something to add on the subject. Tarisio agreed and told Reade of the experimenting that had led him to suspect that Stradivari had used two different types of varnish on his instruments.

Reade laughed. "A fascinating subject on which to speculate," he said. Tarisio's theory was interesting, he continued, and somewhat similar to his own ideas, but not identical. Many violinmakers had tried in vain to fathom Stradivari's formula, and chemists had given countless days and nights of study to the subject, but without success. More than one had thought he had solved the mystery; but when others went to see these new varnishes and compared them with the Stradivari kind, their failure was only too apparent.

"As our British poet Shelley would have put it," Reade said, " 'inextinguishable laughter shook the skies' when Stradivari's varnish and modern discoveries were placed side by side."

Tarisio's eyes twinkled. "Homer said it first in the *Iliad*," he remarked, "and it is a phrase that will live forever. To me nothing could be more apropos to a comparison of Stradivari and nineteenth-century imitators."

Yet Reade, too, was convinced that Stradivari used not one varnish, but two. He was also convinced, he said, that Stradivari first applied two to three coats of a clear oil varnish with a fine gum in suspension, probably a gum widely used in Italy at that time. When this varnish had dried and hardened, he laid on a fourth coat of a heterogeneous varnish consisting of spirit and coloring matter. The red coloring matter was the tear of dragon's blood, little lumps deeper in color than a carbuncle, clear as crystal and fiery as a ruby. When the spirits evaporated, a film of red color was left on the fiddle. Stradivari's yellow coloring, Reade added, was simply the tear of another gum, and some orange effects were achieved by blending the two colors.

Luigi shrugged. "This may be the case," he said, "and perhaps you do have the secret. Who knows?"

"Anyone who follows my directions," Reade cried, "can varnish a violin as beautifully and effectively as any that has come from Cremona!"

Tarisio translated the remark for Vuillaume, and the latter laughed loud and long. "Tell our distinguished vis-

*Antonius Stradivarius, Cremona 1718*

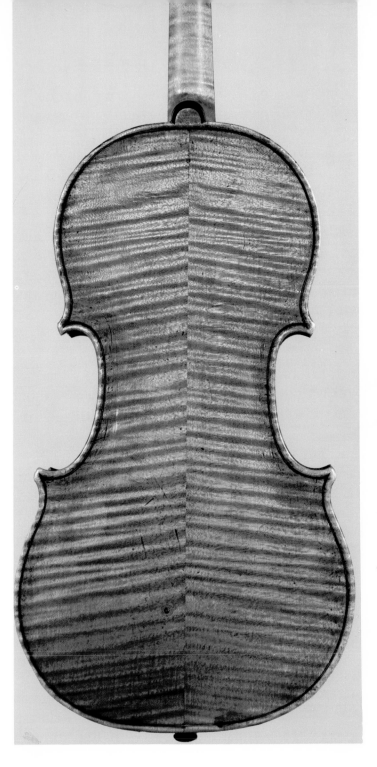

*ex-Arnold Rose, ex-Viotti owned by Robert Mann of Juilliard Quartet*

itor," he said, "that I shall do that very thing. Let us now make a date to meet again in one hundred years and compare results!"

Reade, who understood Vuillaume's French perfectly, joined in the laughter at his expense. "But don't take this too lightly," he admonished. "Someday I shall have more to say on the subject."

Reade had already seen the Bass of Spain, admired its beauty, and heard part of Tarisio's experiences in acquiring it.

"I understand that your ship almost sank on the way back to France."

"Yes," replied Tarisio. "We almost capsized several times."

"Weren't you afraid?"

Tarisio laughed. "I didn't have time to worry about myself. All I was concerned with was Stradivari's masterpiece."

"And not your own safety?"

Tarisio shook his head. "Only the safety of the instrument," he repeated, describing how he had wrapped it in his mattress.

Reade looked at him with admiration, and then remarked: "There is one instrument I particularly wanted to ask you about—Le Messie. Is it true that you have it?"

Tarisio nodded. "It is true."

"And is this violin what everyone believes it is—a work of complete perfection?"

Tarisio nodded again. "I know of no other way to describe it," he said. "It is perfect. But I have news for you. I am retiring from the business of hunting Cremonas. I believe I have found most of them anyway—almost one thousand Cremona instruments have passed through my hands since I first began to search for them. I still have more than two hundred of them in my quarters in Milan. I am going back there very shortly, and I intend to bring them all to Paris—including Le Messie—and turn them over to my friend and benefactor, M. Vuillaume."

The room became as still as a tomb. At last Reade broke the silence. "Is your decision final?"

"It is," Luigi replied, "and I have so informed Vuillaume."

But Tarisio was mistaken. He did not retire then from the business of bringing rare violins to Paris. Thanks to the understanding of Mme. Vuillaume and the help of other friends, he began to recover from the shock of his fiancée's death, and regained some of his former enthusiasm for his vocation. And in 1848, an event occurred that put off his retirement for some years.

In Birmingham, England, an extremely wealthy manufacturer of pens and other writing equipment—Joseph Gillott—had gone to an art gallery to buy a painting. He felt the price was more than the painting was worth, and induced the seller to include some other object of value to even up the transaction. This other object was an old violin, and Gillott was so enchanted with it that he started a collection. Reade, who by now had become known in England as an expert, was called in to help form the collection.

Reade turned to Tarisio for help, and in the next few years a golden tide of precious instruments passed through Reade's hands into the British tycoon's collection. Before he died, some years after Tarisio, Gillott had accumulated the largest collection of Cremona's treasures in all history—more than five hundred; this was more than Tarisio himself had possessed at any one time.

Tarisio knew where these treasures were going, but he did not quarrel with Reade about it. "Perhaps it is best that they rest awhile in Mr. Gillott's museum," he said. "There they will have excellent care, and the day will come when they will be played. Mr. Gillott cannot live forever."

Tarisio was right, but he was dead long before his prediction came true.

*Some of the Strads in the Partello Collection*

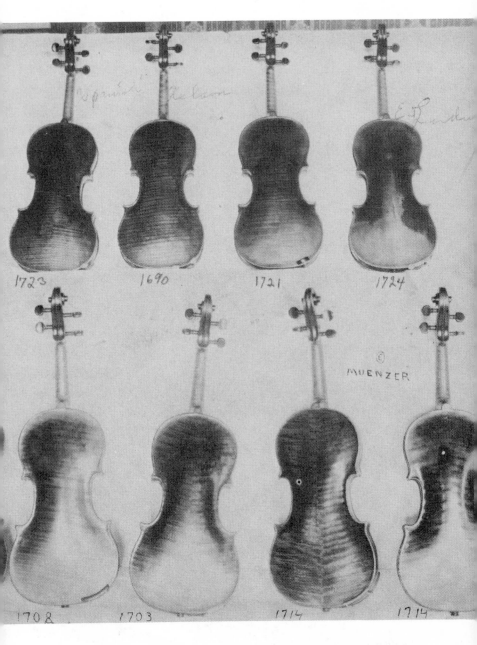

*Backs of Strads in the Partello Collection*

*London in the mid-19th century*

# CHAPTER 26

ALMOST SIX YEARS after Gillott had begun his collection, Reade came to Paris and again met Tarisio at the Vuillaumes' place.

"Your fame has spread to England, and our connoisseurs are anxious to meet you," he said. "Would you do me the honor of coming to England with me?"

Hart and Lott had spoken so glowingly of Tarisio and his work that violin men all over England wanted to meet him. "Besides," Reade insisted, "we have some fine Cremona collections in London, you know."

That decided Tarisio to make the trip. He had made a tremendous impression on the Englishman, and many years later Charles Reade was to write: "The man's whole soul was in fiddles. He was a great dealer, but a greater amateur. He had gems by him no money would buy from him. He was the greatest connoisseur that ever lived or ever can live, because he had the true mind of a connoisseur and vast opportunities."

During the next few days, while the two men traveled to London, Tarisio did his best to satisfy Reade's insatiable curiosity about his life. His parents were quite humble, he said, and unconnected with the musical arts, although his father had learned to appreciate fine violins. In due time he became a carpenter, and eventually acquired a cheap violin, which he taught himself to play.

"I could play a little dance music," he said, "but that was all. I learned how to repair violins by working on that one."

Reade asked Tarisio whether he had ever regretted selling any of the violins he discovered, and Tarisio admitted that he had. Some years earlier he had disposed of a Stradivari in excellent condition to a dealer in Paris. He had been very fond of this particular instrument and longed to see it again. So he made inquiries, and announced his desire to repurchase it should it ever become available. At last his perseverance was rewarded and the instrument was brought to him. Tarisio had been so anxious to see the violin that he could hardly contain himself until the case was opened. He took up the instrument and turned it over and over, devouring the details of its workmanship, when suddenly he groaned in despair. Someone had removed Stradivari's exquisite varnish and put on his own!

"I could never bear to look at it again," he concluded. "The vandal who removed Stradivari's varnish should be quartered and drawn!"

But if Reade found Tarisio's stories absorbing, Luigi was equally fascinated by his host. The Englishman confided some of his own ambitions. "You know," he said, "one day I shall write a great novel about the Middle Ages, for the fifteenth century has always fascinated me."

"An ambitious undertaking," Tarisio said. "What will your story be about?"

"It would take hours to tell you," Reade replied. "But,

briefly, my hero becomes a monk after being falsely led to believe that his sweetheart is dead. Learning in time of the deception, he returns to the world. Through him I hope to recreate the life of his times. I think I shall call it *The Cloister and the Hearth*."

"The church and the people," Tarisio said.

Reade smiled. "In a way," he replied.

The trip to London proved one of the highlights of Tarisio's life. He was received everywhere with respect and admiration. He met John Hart and Lott again, as well as other English makers. He and Reade talked constantly. One afternoon, a day before Tarisio planned to return to Paris, Hart invited Reade and Tarisio to see John Goding's famous collection of stringed instruments. Tarisio had caught cold the night before and tried to beg off, but Reade would not hear of it.

"You simply must see these violins," he urged. "We know you have seen most Cremonas, but these are something extraordinary."

Tarisio finally agreed, and the two started out for John Goding's mansion. The room where the collection was kept was furnished in the most elegant style. The walls were lined with glass cases and shelves upon which the violins rested. Goding led Hart, Reade, and Tarisio to the threshhold with a show of ceremony, and as they reached the door, it was Hart who remarked: "You are about to see England's most precious collection of musical instruments." He bowed, gesturing Tarisio ahead of him.

Goding moved toward his collection and as he did so, Tarisio, standing a good twenty paces away, put on the most amazing demonstration of violin identification the British experts had ever seen. Hart, Reade, and Goding were thunderstruck.

"That's the King Joseph Guarneri," Tarisio cried excitedly, pointing to the first instrument. There was a note of reverence in his voice.

"Among all the violins ever made," Tarisio continued, "with the sole exception of Le Messie, the King Joseph reigns supreme. For majesty of tone, richness of varnish, workmanship, and choice of materials it is Guarneri's greatest masterpiece. It calls for no imagination to see that with this instrument he has made a noble bid for greatness. He fashioned the back from a single piece of maple, cut on the slab. Its figure is brought to life by Guarneri's magnificent varnish. Its voice is without peer."

Still standing in the same spot, Tarisio stretched out a hand and pointed to the second violin. "That is La Font's Guarneri," he went on. "Beside it is a fine Bergonzi. Next are Lord MacDonald's viola, General Kidd's Stradivari, the Marquis de la Rose's Amati, Ole Bull's Guarneri, and the Santo Serafino cello."

"My God—the man must be able to smell the labels," Goding whispered to Reade.

Tarisio had not moved, and Reade, no longer able to contain himself, exclaimed: "How can you identify those instruments without examining them? It must be magic!"

Tarisio smiled and some of his old exuberance showed in his manner. "Gentlemen, you forget that I, of all people, should know these violins—for they are my own children! It was I who found them in the first place."

He stepped to the King Joseph and examined it reverently. Guarneri, he said, had been obsessed with the idea of creating a quality of tone all his own, a tone that combined the sweetness of Amati and the dignity of Stradivari, but with a force and volume almost beyond imagination in his time.

*"The Baltic" by Guarneri del Gesu, 1731*

*The back of "The Baltic"*

"He could foresee," Tarisio went on, "that one day acoustical requirements would call for a great voice. He was a prophet without honor in his own land, but when Paganini came along, his genius was finally recognized. Paganini used a Guarneri, and thus Guarneris became the vogue."

Goding, Hart, and Reade plied the Italian with questions. How had he become so expert a judge? Who had taught him the art of identifying the works of the masters? Where had he studied? To all these questions Tarisio shrugged.

"Vuillaume measures the violins and tests the wood and tries to solve the secret of Cremona scientifically. He discovers new principles of acoustics in these violins, yet he knows that Stradivari knew nothing of acoustics. Guarneri likewise had little general education, and scientific learning.

"These men made violins guided only by instinct and love for their work. I, too, come by my knowledge the same way. I acquired it by instinct, because I love violins."

That evening, upon returning to Reade's quarters, Tarisio announced regretfully that he had best leave England as soon as possible.

"The climate does not agree with me," he complained. "My cold seems much worse."

Reade agreed and after arranging to visit Italy the following summer, he put Tarisio on a boat for France.

Vuillaume had returned from his business trip by the time Tarisio arrived. He greeted him warmly, but, alarmed by his friend's appearance, suggested that he go to bed for a few days.

Vuillaume had just been with Jacques Thibout, the

elderly French violinmaker and dealer, of whom Tarisio was quite fond; next to Vuillaume and Charles Reade, Tarisio admired Thibout most.

"If you don't take care of yourself," Vuillaume said sternly, "I shall tell Thibout how stubborn you are, and you know how caustic he can become."

"That is silly," Tarisio protested. "I have a mere cold. A few days in Italy and I shall be a new man. After all, I have lived outdoors all my life. And frankly, I am quite anxious to return. It has been a long time since I have seen my own family—too long."

There was concern in Vuillaume's face. "You will be careful, won't you?" he entreated. "And you will hurry back?"

Tarisio threw an arm around his friend's shoulders. "Jean Baptiste," he said affectionately, "I shall be back within six weeks—with the greatest, most magnificent collection of Cremona violins the world has ever seen. And they will be right in this very house, in your own loving hands!"

"Just come back in good health," Vuillaume cried, "and damn the violins. One live Tarisio is worth more than all the Cremonas laid end to end!"

Tarisio knew he meant it.

Nostalgia is a vandal which wreaks havoc with some men's lives. It is a knave who whispers lies about yesterday and builds an insidious web around a man's tomorrow. Tarisio sensed that the moment he reached Milan. The city had become a stranger to him. Even the Duomo seemed different. Once it had seemed beautiful, towering over the rest of the city as a symbol of the greatness of faith. Now it appeared to Tarisio as hardly more than a vast network of spires which looked like so many stone fingers pointing skyward.

He was tired and feverish, and his cold was worse. He took a coach to Fontanetto, and soon he stood in front of his home. But Fontanetto was different too, outwardly as well as inwardly. Neighboring buildings seemed even shabbier than they had when he had first bought the place for his parents. His horse and buggy no longer stood behind the house. The horse would long since be dead, he realized, but perhaps the buggy might still be there. He looked in vain for a glimpse of it; all he could see was an old wheel lying in a welter of mud and debris, half covered by a squatting pig.

His sister, who had become stout and gray, opened the door. For a moment he hardly recognized her. All others were strangers too, the surly, skinny boys who eyed him suspiciously, the slovenly man who clung, half dressed, to the kitchen table, noisily drinking tea from a saucer. This was Tarisio's family, his sister, his brother-in-law Giuseppe, and nephews he had never known.

"Well, well, well, so the great man is back!" That came from the kitchen table, and Tarisio merely nodded to his brother-in-law.

"Are you Uncle Stingy?" This came from the tallest of the young boys who dawdled in the kitchen.

From his sister: "Luigi, you are a sight for sore eyes!"

Tarisio stood there, surveying with dismay the crash of his dreams.

"Are you going to stay here?" the smaller boy yelled shrilly. "You won't like it. The place is a mess."

His sister snapped a command. "Giuseppe," she shouted to her husband, "go and make yourself presentable. And you, Joseph and Tony, go clean up instantly."

The grumbling husband and sons shuffled off to obey, and the woman turned to her brother. "Luigi," she said almost tearfully, "I had given up hope of ever seeing you again!" She patted him gently on the cheek. "You are feverish, Luigi," she said. "Go and lie down."

"It is nothing, Sister," he replied. "I caught cold in London recently. It will go away. Tell me, what has happened here?"

Tarisio sat down, and as his sister poured tea for him, she acquainted her brother with the details of the years he had been away. Mama and Papa Tarisio had died within a few weeks of each other, soon after he left. Giuseppe had given up his job and tried to farm grapes and olives. But he was not a farmer. She had written him the news, but Tarisio had never received her letter.

He looked disapprovingly around the house and his sister watched him as his eyes took in the ravages of time and neglect. He mustn't blame Giuseppe, she said, because he knew no better and had no skill, but he did love her and he had been kind to her.

"And the children?"

She shrugged. "They're at an age," she apologized. "If they are not polite it's because they hear other children talk that way and, well, you know how children are."

Tarisio shook his head. "You are a loyal woman, my sister," he said. "Who knows, perhaps someday things will be better for you."

Giuseppe and the boys returned soon after, scrubbed and brushed. At least, Tarisio thought, his sister maintained some semblance of control over her family. At dinner all four asked him questions, and Tarisio talked for hours, regaling his audience with his adventures. That

night, after the boys had been sent to bed, Luigi sat down
with his sister and brother-in-law.

"I have money," he began. "I am going to give you fifty
thousand francs. Get this place in shape. Get some live-
stock, a few pigs, chickens, and enlarge your vineyard. In
time it will pay off."

His sister's eyes were shining. "My brother," she said
softly, "Mama and Papa always said you were wonderful,
and I know that wherever they are, they are happy now."

"And buy some clothing," Tarisio added. "Both of you
need it."

"What do you do next, Luigi?" Giuseppe asked.

Tarisio shrugged. "Who knows? I only know that I am
through chasing after Cremonas. I return to Paris soon
for one last trip. Perhaps I shall settle there. Perhaps I
shall come back here and help farm the land. I really don't
know."

"Come back," Giuseppe said simply. "We need you
here." It was an admission Tarisio had never expected to
hear and it meant much to him. People, he reflected, were
good, and all that a man needed was the patience to wait
for that good to assert itself.

In the morning, for the first time since he had caught
cold, Tarisio realized that he was seriously ill. The fever
parched his throat. He was dizzy and his eyes were burning, but he kept his symptoms to himself. He packed,
determined to go to his place in Milan.

He thought that a voice was calling, a voice that only
he could hear; the voice of his beloved Le Messie. Resolutely he left the house, and an hour later stood in front
of the familiar building in the Via Legnano. He saw the
same dingy restaurant on the ground floor, the same evil
face of the landlord behind the counter. Tarisio walked in

and ordered soup. The man dished up a bowl and remarked: "You've been away a long time."

For a moment fear clutched Tarisio's heart. Had anything happened to his attic and its precious contents?

The man laughed. "Oh," he said, as though he could
read Tarisio's mind, "don't worry. The rent came regularly
by mail and your place has been carefully kept."

His wife walked in. "For the kind of money you have
been sending," she snapped, "I even found time to go up
and dust once in a while."

Tarisio looked at her questioningly.

"Have no fear," the woman reassured him. "Your junk is
safe." She eyed him up and down, noting his clothing and
manicured hands. "And say," she went on, "what does a
fellow like you want with such a hovel and such trash?
Why don't you move into a decent hotel and live like a
gentleman?"

Her husband gave her a furious glance, but she rambled
on unconcerned. "You better find a new place soon," she
said. "The city has bought this land and they will tear it
down one day. The new arena is not far. They have plans
for this property."

Tarisio gulped down his soup. "In a few days, perhaps a
week," he replied slowly, "I shall bid you farewell."

He climbed the steep stairs and they seemed steeper
than ever. Beneath his big coat he was shivering. His fever
was mounting, but as he climbed up on legs of lead he
thought that a little rest would restore his vigor. He hesitated momentarily before he put his key in the lock. Something seemed to stay his hand, but after a few seconds in
the chilly breeze he turned the key and walked in.

Nothing had changed in his beloved little attic. Of all
the places in the world, he reflected, this attic was the

one place that the march of time had passed by. Everything was exactly as he had left it. He ran his eye over his fiddles and smiled. Then he noticed something. There had been a change. The little window in the gable at the far end of the attic had been replaced and closed, and Tarisio smiled happily because it meant that beneath the façade of surliness and hostility of the couple below, there was something else, some kindness. They had closed this window to protect his instruments from the elements. Tarisio was glad, not because it had been a good idea—it wasn't—but simply because they thought enough of him to do it. He lighted a heater and in a few moments the damp chill began to evaporate. He removed his coat, walked to the highboy, pulled open the bottom drawer and took out Le Messie. He had an impulse to put strings on it and play. "I wonder," he asked himself, "what you sound like, what kind of a song you would sing for me?"

But his hands were trembling. He put Le Messie back reluctantly and shut the drawer with unnecessary force. He heard the fiddle slide around. A vague thought disturbed his mind, but he dismissed it.

Walking over to the middle of the line, he took down a Bergonzi and sank into his big chair. He was utterly weary, his eyes burning, their lids heavy. He drifted away into a half-world of slumber and delirium.

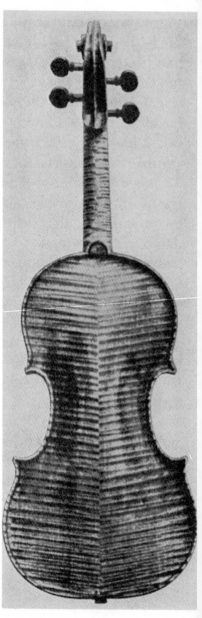

*Violin by Carlo Bergonzi, 1742*

*Engraving titled "The Old Strad"*

*Fountain from Stradivari's house by his tombstone*

# CHAPTER 27

IT IS DOUBTFUL whether Luigi Tarisio knew that death was closing in on him. Coatless and shoeless, he sat in his little apartment, clasping a Bergonzi violin.

What does a man think about when he is dying? In the manner of dreams tinted with delirium, Tarisio's world became a vast stage, across which stretched the whole curtain of time. It rose abruptly, and there was revealed Carlo Bergonzi, his face contorted by a grotesque smile. He shook a finger waggishly at Tarisio. Something seemed to be wrong with this picture. Tarisio should have been a young man sitting eagerly beside the grandson of the unwilling slave of Stradivari. But Tarisio was not young. He was past middle age.

Bergonzi said: "So you did not solve the mystery of Stradivari! I told you long ago you would not."

"I did not seek the secret," Tarisio protested.

Bergonzi smiled wickedly. "But you did," he insisted. "You even found Le Messie and sought to wrest away its secrets. And your friend Vuillaume—he, too, sought the secrets of Stradivari. Does he not copy the Cremona to the last detail, as I did? And do his violins not croak like frogs?"

Tarisio cried out: "I did none of these things. I fulfilled my mission in life."

A tall dark figure walked up behind Bergonzi, and Sister Francesca stood there accusingly, a bitter smile on her lips.

"I trusted you, Tarisio," she said, "and I told you where to find Le Messie. But what have you done with it? Buried it in a musty drawer in a dirty little attic? You promised to restore it to the world, but you have not kept your promise. Le Messie lies hidden where no one will ever find it."

Tarisio's mother spoke humbly to the angry nun: "Sister Francesca, my Luigi is a good boy. You must give him time. He will keep his promise."

"I will, I will," cried Tarisio. "I shall take it to Vuillaume tomorrow, as I have promised."

Large crowds of people appeared on the landscape, people armed with clubs, shovels, pitchforks, and other weapons, and they began to converge on Tarisio. With one hand gripping the Bergonzi, he attempted to shield himself with the other, for long after he had stiffened and become cold, his arm lay across his forehead in a gesture of self-protection.

The scene dissolved. The man who single-handed had restored the lost art of Cremona to the world had himself left the world.

*Violins by Vuillaume, 1847 and 1858*

*Collection of violin-making materials*

# CHAPTER 28

THE DATE WAS January 15, 1855, and in Paris the Vuillaumes were at dinner. It was not a happy occasion, for the Frenchman had been troubled for hours. To his wife across the table he said: "My dear, I have the strangest feeling about Tarisio; a premonition, if you please. Something seems to tell me that all is not well with him."

His wife nodded. "I know, Jean Baptiste," she replied. "I, too, have felt something amiss. We should have had some word from him weeks ago."

Vuillaume leaped to his feet, grimacing at the sudden exertion. "How much cash do we have in our safe?" he asked.

"About fifty thousand francs."

"It's not enough," Vuillaume snapped. "If what I fear has happened to Tarisio, I will need every sou I can put my hands on. Pack two bags for me. I will travel as lightly as I can. I am going out for several hours, and when I return I will leave for Italy at once."

In the next several hours Vuillaume was busier than he

had been in years. From a banker friend whom he persuaded to open his place of business he borrowed fifty
thousand francs, and when he left for Milan he carried on
his person a total of one hundred thousand francs, a fantastic sum to take in cash on a long trip.

In Milan, he sped by coach to Tarisio's address. As they
stopped in front of the restaurant, Vuillaume ordered the
driver to wait, and walked inside.

"I have come from Paris to see Luigi Tarisio," he announced to the proprietor in Italian.

The man shook his head sadly. If Vuillaume wanted to
see Luigi Tarisio he would need supernatural powers;
for, at that moment, the man he sought lay under six feet
of earth in a chestnut grove at Fontanetto. He had been
there almost three months.

Vuillaume was beside himself. What had happened to
his friend? He got the story quickly from the man who had
found the body.

In the neighborhood Tarisio had become a mysterious,
legendary figure, and not even his nearest neighbors had
ever been aware of his true occupation. Generally, Vuillaume was told, Tarisio mounted to his quarters without
exchanging a word with anyone, and always left in the
same taciturn manner. Only the couple who operated the
restaurant suspected his occupation, but they were a close-
mouthed pair who did not discuss it. Tarisio was a good
tenant, a man who always paid his rent in advance for six
months or a year, and they did not wish to incur his displeasure with gossip.

One chilly afternoon late in the preceding October,
neighbors had seen Tarisio go up to his place, and when
several days passed and he was not seen leaving, their
curiosity knew no bounds. They took turns watching, and

by the end of the week the restaurant owner was finally persuaded to notify the municipal authorities. A police officer came, tried Tarisio's door, and found it locked. He reported this to his superior, and received instructions to force an entry.

Thus they found the lifeless body of Luigi Tarisio, sagging in a great chair. Everything around him was in the utmost disorder. Piles of violin cases were stacked everywhere, and violins hung from a long rope that stretched the length of the room. Some hung from the walls, others from the ceiling. Violin backs, bellies, necks, and scrolls were scattered everywhere, together with violin bridges, pegs, fingerboards, and tailpieces. There were at least three huge double basses leaning against a wall, covered with cloth. The officer passed up all this as so much rubbish and began a search for money. He found securities, Italian, French, and English, and evidence that Tarisio not only had invested large sums of money, but also had been generous with loans. The search also yielded a considerable sum in gold coins.

There was one more fact to report. Tarisio had died of congestion of the lungs, and his death had been a natural one.

"But I can tell you one thing," the restaurant man added, "if he had eaten something beside soup and chestnuts he might have had the strength to fight off his illness."

The apartment was sealed and the family at Fontanetto notified. Inasmuch as Tarisio had paid his rent almost a year in advance, the landlord had consented to leave the place as it was until Tarisio's sister could make up her mind about disposing of her brother's possessions. Vuillaume now decided to go to Fontanetto at once to discuss the matter with her.

Many thoughts crowded his mind on the long ride. Where was Le Messie? In what condition were the remaining violins? Would the family try to hold him up? Haste was vital, he realized, for as soon as news of Tarisio's death got around, all Europe would be clamoring for his treasures. Vuillaume, saddened by his friend's death, but concerned over his treasures, urged his driver to greater speed. He wondered idly about Luigi's family, but from what Tarisio had told him, he knew that they were quiet, simple people.

The Frenchman easily recognized Tarisio's sister when she answered his knock; the physical resemblance to his dead friend was remarkable. She had the same deep-blue, wide-set eyes, strong chin and jaw. The recognition was evidently mutual, for Tarisio's sister exclaimed: "You must be M. Vuillaume—it couldn't be anyone else! You know the tragic news?"

Vuillaume nodded. The sister crossed herself and sank into a chair. She never should have permitted her brother to leave, she said, because he had a fever when he first came home; but he had been adamant about going to the Via Legnano, and once he made up his mind nothing could stop him. He had wanted to pack violins and send them to Paris.

"I know," Vuillaume replied, "and that is partly the reason why I am here. He was ill when he left Paris. I came here hoping to persuade him to see a physician. But I came too late."

"What can we do for you now, M. Vuillaume?" the sister asked.

Vuillaume sat down, and at that moment Giuseppe came into the room. He, too, recognized the Frenchman.

"You know," he said, "Luigi has talked of you so much that I would have recognized you anywhere."

The three talked for some time and Tarisio's sister agreed to sell her brother's treasures.

"How much are they worth?" she asked.

"Perhaps as much as seventy-five thousand francs," Vuillaume replied, "if that attic contains what I think it does."

The couple gasped in amazement. To them it was a fortune beyond their fondest dreams.

The three traveled to Milan early the next morning and at once went to the Via Legnano. "So this is where he lived," the sister said, inspecting the building with amazement. "We have never been here, you know."

The three climbed the steep stairs and Vuillaume unlocked the door. He almost fainted when he saw the attic. There were violins everywhere, beautifully varnished creations with the unmistakable stamp of Cremona, scores and scores of them. There was awe in the face of Tarisio's sister. "So this is my brother's legacy; this is what he searched all of Italy to find!"

Vuillaume nodded. "Yes," he replied solemnly, "this is Luigi Tarisio's legacy—the most wonderful one any man could ever hope to leave."

He reached into his breast pocket and took out a bulging billfold. He counted out seventy-five thousand francs and put them triumphantly into the woman's hands. There was stupefaction on her face. Vuillaume, in his agitation at the sight of so many Cremona violins, mistook the look, and acting before she could utter a sound, again dipped into his billfold and counted out another four thousand one hundred and fifty francs.

Giuseppe gasped. His wife stood immobile, but what Vuillaume saw in her eyes this time satisfied him. He quickly scrawled a sentence stating that Tarisio's heirs had sold to him all of Luigi's violins for seventy-nine thousand one hundred and fifty francs, and the couple signed it.

Vuillaume's eyes were moist. His hand trembled as he placed the signed receipt carefully in his pocket, for at that moment, he had become wealthy. He had estimated, simply from a rapid computation, that the violins would eventually fetch a million francs. Within hours he knew that he was right. For in that room he counted two hundred and forty-six of the finest Cremona violins, cellos, and basses the world was ever destined to see.

It was two days before Vuillaume, with hired help, completed the monumental task of packing and cataloguing Tarisio's treasures. But when the job was done, there remained one stunning, disappointing fact: Le Messie was not among them. He slumped into Tarisio's chair in despair. Where was it? Had Tarisio hidden it somewhere else? Had it been stolen? Was it, in fact, merely a figment of his friend's imagination? He stared into space, fixing his eyes on the tall highboy in the corner of the room, and an inspiration came to him. In the excitement of counting and cataloguing the violins, he had completely neglected to search the room. Where else would Tarisio hide his most valuable possession but in the highboy?

He leaped across the room and jerked open the top drawer. It contained nothing but odds and ends, more pegs, fingerboards, and old bridges. Two other drawers were completely empty. In desperation Vuillaume tugged at the bottom drawer, but it refused to budge. He tugged harder, felt something inside shift, and suddenly broke out in a sweat. An inner voice urged him to exercise gentleness and patience.

He toyed with the drawer, probed and tested with delicate movements. At last he pulled again, tentatively. The drawer slid open, and Vuillaume was looking down at Stradivari's masterpiece—Le Messie.

*"Le Messie"*

*St. Domenico before and during its destruction*

# CHAPTER 29

IN 1855 Delphin Alard, Vuillaume's son-in-law, was forty years old and an accomplished violinist. Distinguished and talented, he was also the apple of Vuillaume's eye; it was, therefore, only natural that the older man should choose him to play on Le Messie.

The time was early in March, 1855, a never-to-be-forgotten occasion. Vuillaume had called in his friends to see Tarisio's treasures, and then he brought out Le Messie. This most famous of all violins was about to be played for the first time—in the knowledge of any living being—since its creation in 1716.

Delphin Alard rosined his bow. Vuillaume spoke, to no one in particular, perhaps to his dead friend Luigi Tarisio.

"Since the day it was made in 1716, this masterpiece has been silent. It has never known the touch of a bow. What will it say as my son-in-law draws his bow across the strings?" But in his heart he knew what the voice of Le Messie would sound like.

He was not disappointed. Alard's bow glided across the strings, and the imprisoned soul of Le Messie sang out

*"Le Messie"* (Ashmolean Museum, Oxford England)

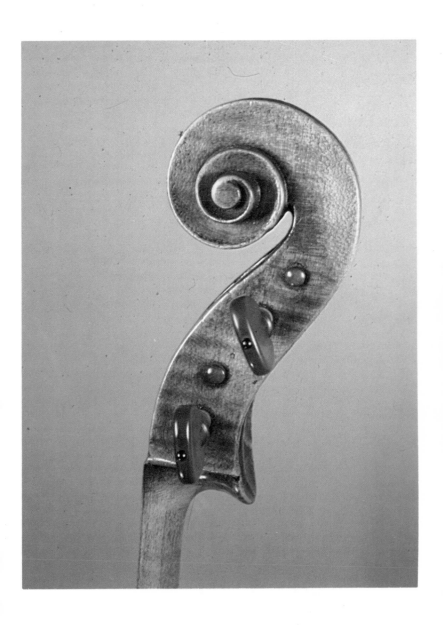

*The perfection of a Stradivari scroll as exemplified by the inlaid viola shown on the two pages following page 107. Photograph by Isabelle Francais.*

in great, joyful tones. Alard played and the Messiah sang, weaving a magic spell over all within its hearing.

When Alard was finished, amid the silent admiration of his hearers, he handed Le Messie back to his father-in-law, who tenderly packed it away again.

It had been an epochal event: for Le Messie was never again played by a professional artist. After Vuillaume died the instrument passed through various hands and eventually was acquired by William Ebsworth Hill of London. After his death it was placed in the Hill Room of the Ashmolean Museum in Oxford, England. There it rests today in a specially designed glass case—the most perfect example of the highest skill ever achieved in the evolution of the violin.

Its value? No one knows; for who can put a price tag upon the voice of the angels, upon the quintessence of Stradivari's soul?

# EPILOGUE

The instrument on which he played
Was in Cremona's workshops made.
By a great master of the past,
Ere yet was lost the art divine;
Fashioned of maple and of pine,
That in Tyrolean forests vast
Had rocked and wrestled with the blast,
Exquisite was it in design,
A marvel of the lutist's art,
Perfect in each minutest part!
And in its hollow chamber, thus,
The maker from whose hands it came
Had written his unrivalled name
Antonio Stradivarius.

> From *Tales of a Wayside Inn*
> by Henry Wadsworth Longfellow

BY 1869 Luigi Tarisio had been dead for fifteen years, and his modest grave at Fontanetto was overgrown with weeds and forgotten, because the loving hands of those near to him also had been stilled by death.

But in London, Paris, Brussels, Berlin, New York, and Philadelphia the heavenly creations Tarisio had rescued

*J.B. Guadagnini, Turin 1773*

*ex-Campoli, ex-Grumiaux owned by Joseph Silverstein*

already were being assembled into fabulous collections. Wealthy men and women paid thousands of dollars for violins Tarisio had sold, in some cases, for a few francs.

Music lovers from everywhere came to the ancient city of Cremona to see the house where Stradivari had lived and worked, and to walk the street once trod by the feet of such illustrious men as Stradivari, his sons, the Amatis, the Guarneris, the Bergonzis, Guadagnini, and the others.

The people of Cremona could not understand this. Across the street from the building at which the visitors gaped—a modernized version of Stradivari's home—stood the church of San Domenico, and for almost one hundred years there had been talk of tearing it down. It mattered little to Cremona that the mortal remains of the most famous name in this nearly a thousand-year-old city rested there. It mattered little that people came to take pictures, or to pray, or to stand and talk in reverent tones and to marvel at the skill of these violinmakers. The church of San Domenico was an eyesore. It had fallen into decay, as had many of Italy's noble monuments, and was therefore dangerous.

In 1729 Stradivari had already decided on his burial place, and from the heirs of Fancesco Villani, descendant of a noble Cremonese family, he bought their tomb, situated in a small chapel named for the Blessed Virgin, in San Domenico. With his own hands he carved the name Stradivari on the stone marker, obliterating the name of the original owner.

In March of 1737, Stradivari's second wife died and was buried there, to be followed by her husband on December 18th of the same year.

A church record reads: *In the year of our Lord one*

*thousand seven hundred and thirty-seven, on the nine-
teenth day of the month of December, Signor Antonio
Stradivari, a widower, aged about ninety-five years, having died yesterday, fortified by the holy sacraments and
comforted by prayers for his soul until the moment he
expired, I, Domenico Antonio Stancari, parish priest of
this church of Saint Matteo, have escorted today his
corpse with funeral pomp to the church of the very reverend fathers of Saint Domenico in Cremona, where he was
buried.*

From time to time other Stradivaris were buried there,
the last being a son, Giuseppe Antonio, who died in 1781.

Now, in 1869, the venerable church was so run down
that it offended the estheticism of Cremona. A few of the
older people spoke wistfully of restoring the building, but
nobody listened to them. Cremona was practical. The
church site would make a fine public garden, a place
where people could come to relax from their labors.

In the spring of 1869 the decision to raze the church
was finally taken by the officials of Cremona. Workmen
armed with picks, shovels, and sledge-hammers began to
attack it. First the great apses, the towers, and the chapel
of Christ disappeared. All day long, day in and day out,
the dull pounding of the sledge-hammers echoed through
the street. Wagon-load after wagon-load of debris was
hauled away. A cupola by Malosso and a ceiling by
Cattapane came tumbling down, and the work of the
wreckers went on remorselessly. Aurelio Betri, the town
photographer, came around to get "action pictures" of the
devastation.

When the workmen came to the tombs, a handful of
Cremona's elder statesmen gathered to consider what
should be done. There was a lawyer by the name of

*Antonius Stradivarius, Cremona 1709*

*ex-Ernst, ex-Lady Halle, owned by Wm. Kroll*

Tavolotti; the mayor; a physician, Dr. Robolotti; Professor Bissolati, a librarian; Professor Peter Fecit, also a librarian. Several times the name of Stradivari was mentioned.

Someone said: "By now there is such a confusion of bones without any special mark that it seems useless to search."

A special group of men was put to work, equipped with baskets and assigned one task: to gather up the bones of Cremona's past. Skulls, tibias, ribs, thigh bones, bones of arms, hands, and feet began to fill the baskets. But no attempt was made to sort them into individual skeletons. The Cremonese gentlemen who directed the wrecking job, Ferdinando Rossi and Francisco Ferrari, saved a few skulls for souvenirs. Perhaps they had the skull of one of Cremona's heroes, perhaps the skull of Stradivari himself. But what did it matter? They were dead, were they not? And didn't the priest always remark that the body was as nothing without a soul? A few miles out of town other workmen had dug a huge hole, and into this, commingled with the bones of others, went those of Antonio Stradivari.

After a while, the enormity of the offense struck home and the city council of Cremona found enough money to erect a monument. Later on, in the street where Stradivari had labored, a plaque was placed on the wall of the building:

HERE STOOD THE HOUSE IN WHICH ANTONIO STRADIVARI
BROUGHT THE VIOLIN TO ITS HIGHEST PERFECTION AND
LEFT TO CREMONA AN IMPERISHABLE NAME AS MASTER
OF HIS CRAFT

This, then, was Cremona's tribute to its famous native son.

But it was left to a foreigner to write a fitting epitaph

to Cremona's genius. Vuillaume's friend, Fetis, finally
wrote his book and he said this of the immortal violinmaker:

> Stradivari was one of those few men who, in aiming at per-
> fection, so far as it is possible for humanity to attain it,
> never swerve from the path which may conduct them
> thereto: men who suffer nothing to divert or turn them aside
> from their object; who are not discouraged by fallacies, but
> who, full of faith in the value of the object they have in
> view, as well as in their ability for its realization, contin-
> ually recommence that which they have done well, in order
> to arrive at the best possible result. To Stradivari the mak-
> ing of stringed instruments was the whole world; thereon
> he concentrated his entire self. In this way only can a man
> raise himself, when aptitude answers to the will.

Luigi Tarisio restored the lost art of Cremona and
thereby gave future composers and performers the means
to express their art to perfection.

When Antonio Stradivari died, an incomparable era
came to an end. The Piazza San Domenico, where he, the
Amatis, Joseph Guarneri del Gesu, Bergonzi, and others
had labored side by side in their own shops, quickly became a street of memories. They had made thousands of
fine violins—Stradivari alone more than one thousand—but
one day, in the early years of the nineteenth century, the
world awakened to the realization that the whereabouts
of fewer than fifty were known.

What had happened to the wonderful instruments of
Stradivari and his contemporaries? All of Europe asked
that question. It was ironic, but the one living person who
knew the answer was the naïve, self-educated handy man,
carpenter and fiddler, Luigi Tarisio. Into nearly every little
city and village went this determined young man. Church-
men knew him in the cathedrals and monasteries of Milan,

*Joseph Guarnerius del Gesu, Cremona 1740*

*ex-Ysaye, owned by Isaac Stern*

Mantua, Bergamo, Chivasso, Cuneo, Mondori, Tortoni, Parma, Verona, and Brescia, and the peasants came to know him in the farms and town halls of Italy. His quest even opened the doors to the castles of many noble Italian families and to the salons of eminent artists. Tarisio dedicated his life to his search, and the result was one of the truly remarkable achievements of recent times. In the span of approximately twenty-seven years, he found more than one thousand priceless Cremona violins, cellos, and bass fiddles and sent them on their way to the concert halls of the world. As a result, he is entitled to a share in the glory of Paganini, Heifetz, Ysae, Milstein, Menuhin, Francescatti, Ole Bull, Albert Spalding, Maude Powell, Elman, Kreisler, and many others. For of what avail would be Raphael's artistry without paint, brush, or canvas?

Although Tarisio was ignored by his contemporaries, and by history, the effect of his work is so great that even today—more than one hundred years after his death—its result seems almost as important as the art he rediscovered.

Much of the pedigree of old violins originates with Tarisio; few indeed are the Cremonas which can be traced directly to the hands of their makers. For example, the violin known as the Red Diamond, one of the finest specimens of Stradivari's greatest period, owes its pedigree to Tarisio. Named for the color of its rich varnish, the Red Diamond, made in 1732, was found by Tarisio in the storeroom of an Italian church. He brought it to Paris and sold it to Vuillaume. In 1860 Vuillaume sold it to a professor at the Paris Conservatoire. The professor—a man named Herwyn—later sold it to George Haddock. Haddock sold it to George Hart, the famous English connoisseur and son of John Hart, who cherished it until he died. Then a Scottish nobleman acquired the Red Diamond, but he later returned it to Hart's sons, the firm of Hart and Son. In 1918 they sold it to Francis Jay Underhill, a Brooklyn bond broker. Emil Herrmann bought the Red Diamond from Underhill, and in 1937 it passed to a group of Baltimore music patrons.

Another famous violin found by Tarisio was the Naduad, which has a beautiful two-piece back of broad-figured maple, richly varnished with a red-brown color. Tarisio brought the Naduad to Paris. Eventually it was acquired by the renowned violin teacher and artist Edouard Naduad, for whom it was named. Naduad possessed it until 1909, then Willy Burmester, and then Hamma & Company of Stuttgart, who sold it to George Kuhlemkampff, concertmaster of the Bremen Philharmonic Orchestra.

The Frenchman Gand was the fortunate man who acquired from Tarisio the Muntz Stradivari, said to be second only to Le Messie in beauty and perfection. In an historical sense alone, the Muntz probably was Tarisio's greatest discovery, for this violin is the one that definitely established Stradivari's age. The Muntz was created in 1736, and in his own handwriting, the Raphael of Cremona wrote his age in the label: "D'anni 92." The Muntz is the only written proof existing of Stradivari's age. It passed from Stradivari's shop to his son Paolo, then to Count Cozio di Salabue. Tarisio got it from Di Salabue on his historic mission to Florence when he also acquired Le Messie.

In the collection of fine instruments at the Paris Con-

*Joseph Guarnerius del Gesu, Cremona 1733*

*ex-Kreisler, owned by Library of Congress*

servatoire is one of the few *pochettes*—dance-masters' fiddles—made by Stradivari. Such a violin is narrow and easily carried under a player's coat. Tarisio brought it to France, selling it to Pierre Sylvestre, of Lyon, where he frequently stopped to rest on his journeys.

It is known that Tarisio was responsible for other now famous instruments—the Pressardi Stradivari, the Hegar cello, the Hart cello, the Goding Amati, the Hawley Maggini (made in 1615, and believed to be the oldest violin in existence), the Tarisio Bergonzi, the Hawley Rogeri, the priceless Bass of Spain, the Pawle cello, the King Joseph Guarneri, Lord MacDonald's Stradivari viola, and hundreds of others. And no one knows how many instruments whose pedigrees begin with Vuillaume and Hart were actually found by Tarisio. In addition to the Stradivaris and Guarneris, the list of violins of lesser makers recovered by Tarisio is almost endless.

Tarisio always kept a watchful eye on people who possessed rare violins but would not part with them. He haunted the Mantuan family of Antonio Bonazzi for years. A violinist of independent means, Bonazzi collected Cremonas. He was one of the few men of his time in Italy who appreciated their beauty; and at his death in 1802, he had left 42 fine instruments—Stradivaris, Guarneris, Amatis, and others—valued then at 3,000 pounds, British. But the family would not sell to Tarisio. Vuillaume knew of this gold mine, for Tarisio had told him about it, but whether he ever tapped it after Tarisio died is unknown to me.

Tarisio's career was an inspiration. As a collector and dealer, he gained great wealth, but it was not the wealth that drew him on. He pursued a dream. And if there was any real tragedy in his life, it was that he missed hearing Le Messie played by Delphin Alard, the famed Parisian violinist and son-in-law of Vuillaume, when it first appeared in Paris, more than a century after Stradivari made it. However, it is not too difficult to believe that Luigi Tarisio could hear the glorious voice of Le Messie merely by looking at it; because between him and violins there was an affinity far beyond ordinary understanding.

My search for Luigi Tarisio has been painstaking and persevering, and often exciting. I have hunted him for more than a decade in the literature, lore, and records of a dozen countries, and examined more than twenty million words in hundreds of books, essays, letters, monographs, novels, and memoirs. I have delved in public and private libraries in a score of cities, written letters to people all over the world, and penetrated the scarcely legible records of numerous churches in Italy through the entire history of a great era in art—1600 to 1900 A.D. Dealers all over Europe have received my question: "Can you trace any of the rare Cremonas you have handled to Luigi Tarisio?"

Sometimes the results of the research, the answers to the letters, have been satisfying, often disappointing. But out of all has come a picture of a man who deserves to be ranked alongside Cremona's greatest craftsmen. He was a self-taught man whose gifted tongue knew all of the Italian dialects and a touch of French, Spanish, and English; a man envied by many but known by few; a man who slipped suddenly back into the obscurity from which he had come.

There are no statues to Luigi Tarisio, no plaques, no monuments. His only epitaph is a chance remark that

*Antonious Stradivarius, Cremona 1728*

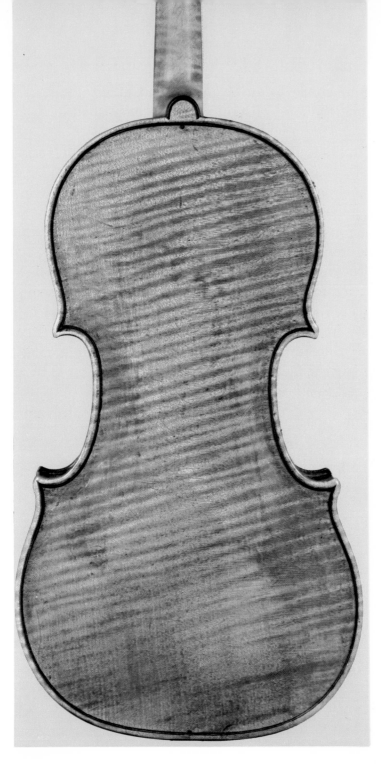

*The Hart, owned by Zino Francescatti*

Paganini made to an English friend about Tarisio: "Of him one can say: Mission in life accomplished."

I have one regret about my reconstruction of Tarisio's life, and that is that I have to give the woman he loved a fictitious name. History does not identify her. I have invented the name Countess Margaretta Duero; but she was a living person and the story of the Bass of Spain, in which she figures, is true.

With the exception of some of the dialogue, which I have used to help define the presumed motives of some of the people in it, this story has been reconstructed in its entirety from historical fact. Even of the dialogue, a considerable amount is documented; the rest might rank as reconstructed fact, being based on stories repeated by the principals to others.

William Alexander Silverman

# INDEX

*"The Baltic," Guarnerius del Gesu, 1731 (Photography by Violin Reflections of Harry A. Duffy Violins, Incorporated)*

*Back view of "The Baltic" (Photography by Violin Reflections of Harry A. Duffy Violins, Incorporated)*